PENGUIN COMPASS

ARE YOU SMARTER THAN YOU THINK?

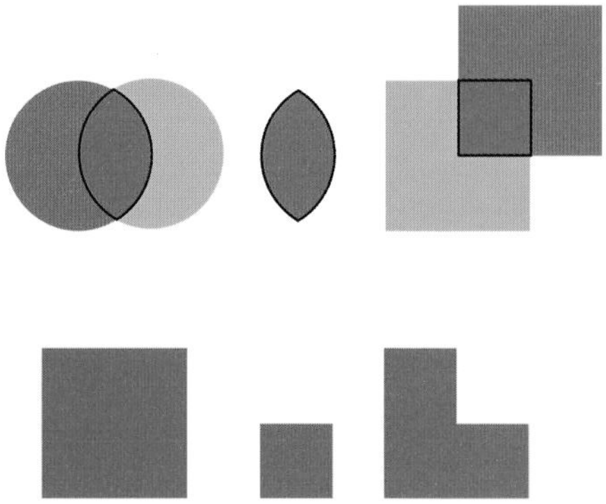

Claire Gordon is an expert in the complementary fields of health and psychology. She has worked as Head of Health and Social Care at NFER-NELSON (a psychometric assessment publisher), where she researched and developed intelligence and emotional assessments for adults and children. Claire has also adapted educational, occupational, and clinical test batteries from the United States for the Psychological Corporation (part of Harcourt International).

ARE YOU SMARTER THAN YOU THINK?

160 ways to test and enhance your **natural intelligence**

CLAIRE GORDON

PENGUIN COMPASS

TO CHRIS AND BETH, WITH LOVE

PENGUIN BOOKS
Published by the Penguin Group
Penguin Group (USA) Inc., 375 Hudson Street,New York, New York 10014, U.S.A.
Penguin Books Ltd, 80 Strand, London WC2R 0RL, England
Penguin Books Australia Ltd, 250 Camberwell Road,Camberwell, Victoria 3124, Australia
Penguin Books Canada Ltd, 10 Alcorn Avenue,Toronto, Ontario, Canada M4V 3B2
Penguin Books India (P) Ltd, 11 Community Centre,Panchsheel Park, New Delhi—110 017, India
Penguin Books (N.Z.) Ltd, Cnr Rosedale and Airborne Roads, Albany, Auckland, New Zealand
Penguin Books (South Africa) (Pty) Ltd, 24 Sturdee Avenue, Rosebank, Johannesburg 2196, South Africa
Penguin Books Ltd, Registered Offices: 80 Strand, London WC2R 0RL, England

First published in Great Britain by Carroll & Brown Limited 2003
Published in Penguin Books 2004

1 3 5 7 9 10 8 6 4 2

CARROLL & BROWN LIMITED
20 Lonsdale Road
London NW6 6RD

Project Editor **Anna Amari-Parker**
Art Director **Frank Cawley**

LIBRARY OF CONGRESS CATALOGING-IN-PUBLICATION DATA
Gordon, Claire, 1968–
Are you smarter than you think?/Claire Gordon.
p. cm
Includes biographical references and index.
ISBN 0-14-200321-2
1. Multiple intelligences. I. Title
BF432.3.G67 2004
153.9—DC21 2003043864
Printed in Singapore by Imago

Contents

What is INTELLIGENCE?

A single definition of intelligence has eluded psychologists for nearly a century, yet this is the area of psychology most extensively researched. It is not simply of academic interest either, since we have probably all come across intelligence tests of one sort or another at some point during our lives.

Some animal species are naturally "smarter" than others. Dogs, dolphins, and monkeys, for example, can be trained to perform complex and demanding tasks completely beyond the ability of other species like sheep or fish, while humans are more intelligent than even the cleverest of chimpanzees. Variations in intellectual ability also occur within humans.

Psychologists have been divided between those who view intelligence as a general core ability, and those who believe it to be composed of a number of distinct and separate factors. Intuitively, we recognize that some people are more intellectual, verbally adept, musically gifted, or artistic than their peers.

In its purest sense, intelligence is understood to be the cognitive ability to understand events or information, then process this information rationally in order to respond appropriately to what is happening around us. Broader theories of intelligence (like Howard Gardner's multiple intelligence theory) go beyond pure brainpower and encompass the brain's ability to interact with the whole body.

Our brains represent the source of intelligent thought and action. An individual brain consists of between eight to 10 billion nerve cells, each of which has between 1,000 and 10,000 connections to other neurones. What is unusual about human brains is that a large proportion of these connections are not devoted to physical or physiological functions, and are therefore left "free" for learning, communicating, thinking, remembering, and reasoning.

The brain is divided into three concentric layers:

- The central core, which controls balance and smooth muscle movement, the sense organs, and regulates metabolism;
- The limbic system, which is concerned with satisfying basic needs and instincts;
- The cerebrum, where sensations are registered, is also dedicated to the processing of higher mental functions like voluntary actions, decision-making, and the formulation of plans.

Although each brain area has specialized functions, it still interacts with other sections. The cerebrum wraps around the central core and the limbic system, and is more developed in humans than in any other species. Its outer layer is called the cerebral cortex. It has a folded and wrinkled appearance and the term "gray matter" comes from its color. It is divided into two separate hemispheres, which look like mirror images of each other, yet have very different functions.

Sight, hearing, touch, smell, and taste are processed by specific areas of the cerebral cortex present on both sides of the brain. The remainder of the cortex (about three-quarters) is concerned with intelligence, memory, learning, and language, but such functions are hemisphere-specific.

The left hemisphere generally controls written and spoken language, mathematical calculation, and complex logical and analytical activities. The right hemisphere has limited language and mathematical capabilities, but excels at spatial ability and non-verbal reasoning. It can construct geometric and perspective drawings, and identify faces and facial expressions.

In reality, all parts of the brain interact with one another as one unit. The brain is an extraordinary tool, and humans have been granted the gift of supreme intelligence over all other species. The opportunity to maximize this potential lies ahead of you and is well within your control.

THE HUMAN BRAIN (SURFACE AND MIDLINE VIEW)

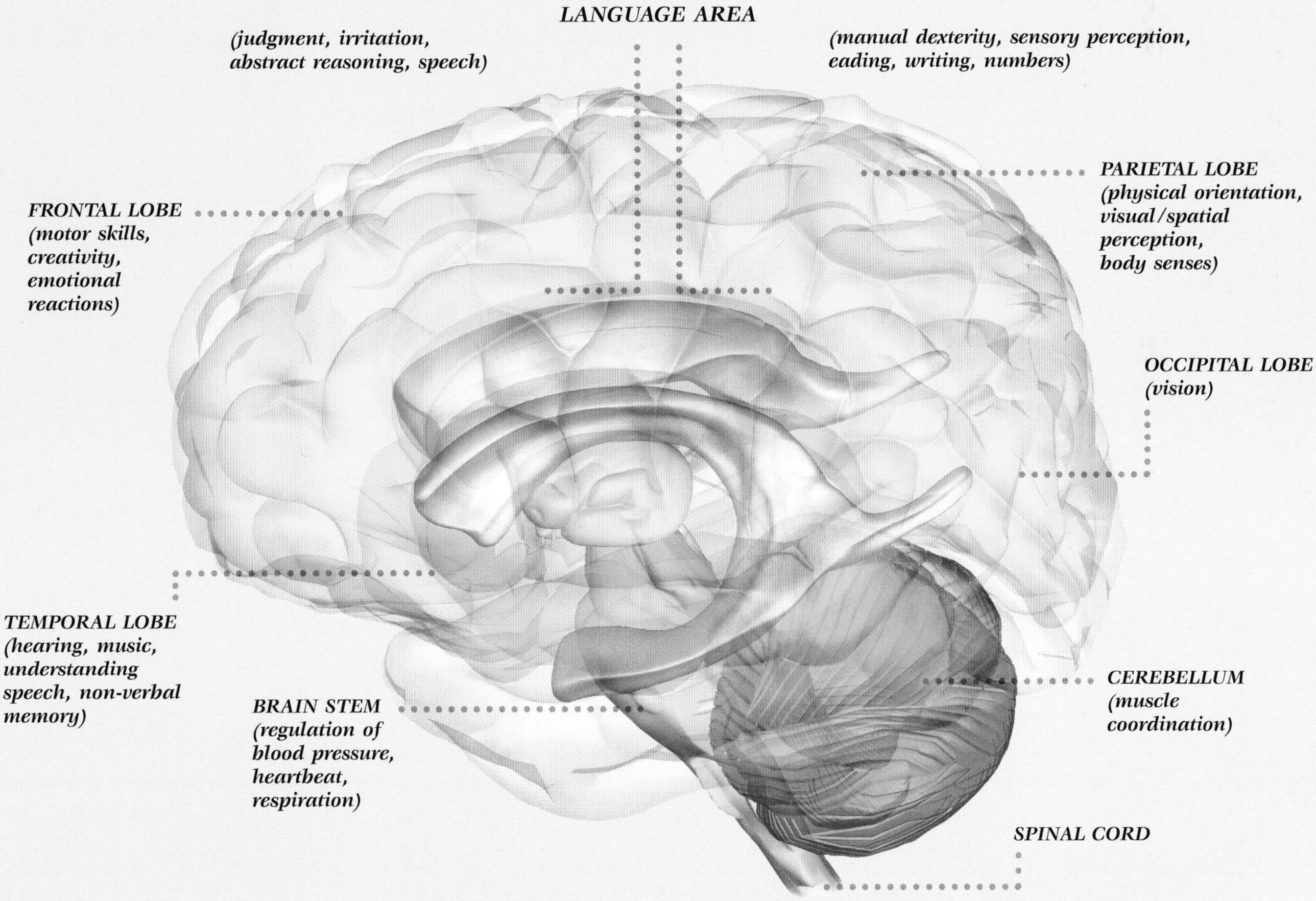

INTELLIGENCE: nature or nurture?

We know intuitively that people differ in terms of their intelligence profiles—some excel where others struggle and vice versa. One of the great intelligence theory debates centers around whether such differences are largely due to our genetic make-up, and are therefore a fixed part of our biological nature, or whether environmental factors and the way we are nurtured have the final say on our "intelligence outcome."

Nature: our genes

As a unique blueprint of our DNA, genes act as a permanent template for basic and higher body functions. We cannot change our DNA—it is a singular, one-off combination of our parent's genes. Geneticists believe that these heredity units are very significant in determining our intelligence profile. This is supported by research showing that identical twins (who have the same DNA profile and very similar nurturing) are more likely to display the same IQ score than non-identical twins (who are genetically different yet have also been raised together).

These genetic arguments for intelligence have sometimes been misused to promote racist theories of intellectual supremacy because environmental factors are often discounted by geneticists as the reason for significantly lower IQ scores among certain racial groups. The vast majority of psychologists, however, do not sweep aside nurture evidence such as:

- Differences in school performance that can be virtually eliminated by intensive tutoring;
- A normal college student who is able to increase his short-term memory by tenfold;
- An average Japanese child who can become a protégé violinist using the Suzuki Method.

Common sense, and scientific evidence, point to the crucial role of nurturing and the environment.

Nurture: our environment

While some individual differences are due to genetics, the environment in which we grow up can radically influence our intelligence potential. Environmental factors influence our experiences in the womb as well as after we are born. Issues such as the home environment we grow up in, family and school moves, absence from school, nutrition, cultural values, and general health all affect intelligence. Consider two children with the same genes—the child who receives better nutrition (before and after birth), more intellectual stimulation, emotional security at home, and encouragement at school, will score a higher IQ.

Headstart programs focus resources on helping underprivileged preschoolers and have been shown to have significantly positive impacts on later school performance. Those programs that involved and engaged parents the most produced the best overall results. Parents play a crucial role in developing a child's intelligence.

Personal traits can also affect intelligence. For example, a challenging environment may boost your IQ, but your score could drop again were circumstances around you to suddenly change. People who are naturally a bit more intelligent may seek more challenging situations, which will encourage them to become even smarter. IQ scores may be influenced by idiosyncratic factors such as enthusiasm, concentration, energy levels, previous experience of the testing process, and self-confidence.

Developing intelligence

As a consequence, we will never be in a position to have to choose nature over nurture or the other way around: both are equally important. You may have felt you were born with a certain level of intellect, and that you have simply had to make do with what you were given. The great news is that your intelligence can be shaped, challenged, and increased through day-to-day events and experiences if you choose to seek these out.

There are individual differences in the intellectual profiles of children and adults. Even if different members of the same family receive consistently high-quality nurturing and stimulation, individual strengths and weaknesses will still exist. Scientists still have much to learn and discover about how intelligence is really made up, what influences it most, and what is of less consequence. You will undoubtedly come to hear more in the future about how nature and nurture work together to shape the brain and human intelligence.

MULTIPLE intelligence theory

UP UNTIL THE 1980s, the general view was that there was only one kind of intelligence, which remained fixed at the same level from birth throughout our lives. This stance was challenged by Harvard-educated professor Howard Gardner in his groundbreaking book, *Frames of Mind: The Theory of Multiple Intelligence* (1983). Its impact on academic, educational, and public audiences was unparalleled. After extensive research, Gardner concluded that there were at least six different types of intelligence, which could be developed individually, challenging the viewpoint that it could (and should) be summed up in a single IQ score. The inclusive and positive nature of his theory has contributed to its enduring popularity and relevance.

What are the multiple intelligences?

You are likely to have come across these two types of "core" intelligence already because they are measured as IQ at school:

- Numerical—the ability to use numbers effectively, and deduce, reason, and apply logic;
- Linguistic—the capacity to use words effectively, in speaking or writing.

There are more specialized "extensions" as well:

- Musical—the capability to perceive, transform, and express musical forms;
- Spatial—the skill to recognize and manipulate objects or images in space;
- Physical—the physical expertise required to move the body for self-expression or to produce objects.

Lastly, there is one final category of intelligence, the most unusual one for intelligence theory:

- Personal—the ability to understand and manage one's own feelings and those of others.

Gardner always maintained that, although he initially found there to be only six types of intelligence to fit his strict scientific criteria, there could well be more. He has since recognized naturalistic intelligence, for example, and defined it as the ability to recognize and classify plants, animals, and other natural phenomena.

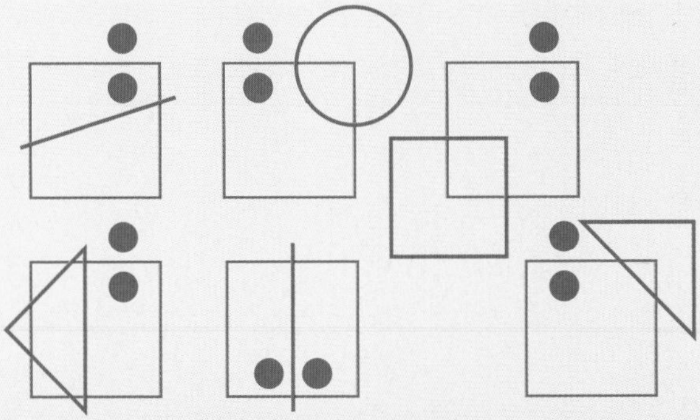

In this book, some types of intelligence have been divided into sub-categories so readers can explore specific facets more thoroughly: conceptual and mathematical intelligence, for example, are covered in separate chapters; in keeping with emotional intelligence theory, personal intelligence has been sub-divided into *inter*personal and *intra*personal.

What is multiple intelligence theory?

Every individual possesses all seven types of intelligence to varying degrees. We all, for instance, have some level of musical ability—some of us are so gifted we can actually compose music whereas others just love rhythm.

Most people are able to achieve a respectable level of competency for every type of intelligence if given adequate encouragement and instruction. Multiple intelligence theory holds that you're not stuck with the intelligence profile you were born with. Once you are able to identify key strengths, you can then use them to your advantage in your individual quest for self-improvement, knowledge, and development.

There are many ways to be smart within each type of intelligence. You can be linguistically intelligent and an amazing storyteller but you may not be able to read. Or you might be lousy at sports, but a talented sculptor. Different types of intelligence interact in complex ways and don't exist in isolation: a professional footballer, for example, needs spatial as well as physical intelligence to coordinate his body movements and interact well with the ball if he is to pass it accurately.

What are the implications?

Multiple intelligence theory (MIT) goes beyond a psychological profile of intellectual abilities. It recognizes that while we all have strengths and weaknesses, we can improve by working on our weaknesses. One of the most positive aspects of MIT is its role in teaching and learning. Some schools have embraced MIT and children are taught topics in ways that appeal to their individual strengths. For example, if a class is learning about President Abraham Lincoln, they might be asked to compose a song about him (using musical intelligence), write a play about the events in his life (stimulating linguistic intelligence), act them out as a group (activating physical intelligence), or draw an annotated picture (encouraging spatial intelligence).

As adults, we maximize our learning opportunities by using individual strengths to gain knowledge and MIT provides us with the necessary tools. Imagine you want to learn a new software program. If you are linguistically intelligent, you might read the manual, or ask a colleague familiar with the program to give you a practical demonstration and draw on your personal intelligence. You might also want to sketch a flow chart of the screens you need to navigate through using your spatial aptitude.

Each one of us is intelligent in one way or another and we need to develop our potential intelligence, so that we can implement a framework for learning and developing in daily living that fits with our own individual strengths.

1

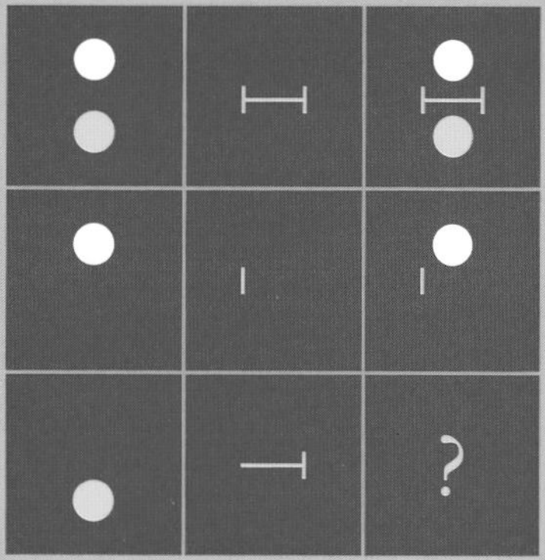

CONCEPTUAL

INTELLIGENCE

What is conceptual intelligence?

Everyone organizes his or her thoughts in keeping with some kind of logic. We apply reasoning to gather our observations, deduce future outcomes, and plan our actions. If the sky looks overcast, experience leads you to conclude it might rain. You don't want to get wet, so you take an umbrella or raincoat with you when you go outside. You have thought through a given situation to reach a distinct conclusion, even if you weren't consciously aware of the individual thought processes that got you there. This "thinking through" is pure conceptual intelligence which breaks down into logical, spatial, and abstract reasoning.

Logical reasoning

Children start to truly develop logical thinking at around the age of seven, with experimental findings showing that toddlers can order and classify objects even if only by color and size. Adult logical reasoning extends this skill to thinking hypothetically, considering possibilities and other viewpoints, and ordering or assessing thoughts, ideas, and information. It often helps to have some experience of life because the ability to build on and question your

existing knowledge base is key, and logical reasoning is often tested using random symbols in patterns or sequences. This ensures fairer testing methods as everyone is working with unfamiliar material.

Spatial reasoning

Three related aptitudes—recognizing and mentally manipulating three-dimensional objects from different angles, generating and altering mental imagery, and producing a graphic likeness of objects—fall within the domain of spatial reasoning. These processes have been employed throughout history by scientists and artists alike: the ultimate example being Leonardo da Vinci, the Renaissance artist, whose groundbreaking anatomical drawings and scientific sketches were incontestable indications of his phenomenal spatial genius.

Abstract reasoning

Perceived to be one of the fairest forms of intelligence testing, being able to see patterns and relationships between objects does not rely on previous experience—even with something as apparently universal as numbers. The ability to reason around abstract concepts is viewed as one of the highest (and hence most difficult) forms of logic and science. Abstract reasoning often involves high degrees of creative, right-brained mental activity to spot a pattern or existing order before applying logical, right-brained thought processes.

Why is conceptual intelligence important?

Human beings differ from other animals in that we are able to reason, think logically, and deduce. Such skills have enabled us to influence, manage, and transform our surrounding world to such an extent that the importance of reasoning in everyday life has resulted in the rise of conceptual intelligence as both an indicator and a measure of IQ.

People who possess a high degree of conceptual intelligence are naturally inclined to appreciate art; they can visualize and manipulate three-dimensional objects with ease; enjoy doing puzzles and imagining or figuring out mazes. They readily perceive the relationships of physical objects in space. Equally they are adept at problem-solving, classifying and categorizing information, working with abstract concepts to figure out links, designing and conducting experiments, questioning, and working out natural events. Such individuals often have an easy time with subjects like geometry or geography at school, and tend to shine in the visual arts including photography, sculpture, and architecture. Other examples of suitable professions for people who excel in this area include computer programming, design, various branches of science, research, and the medical and legal professions.

Do you think logically?

LOGICAL ABILITY REFERS to the capacity to make and see patterns and relationships from individual pieces of information. Most often associated with scientific thinking, this skill is highly valued in our education system and Western culture as a whole.

It may be tested theoretically without using language or meaningful symbols, so that the test-taker is forced to employ logic in its purest sense. But what about logical reasoning in real life? What advantages does it confer to a person with the ability to think deductively using reason?

The essence of being logical is characterized by the ability to problem-solve. Every one of us, each and every day of our lives, is presented with problems. To solve these "problems," which could involve anything from juggling a crowded schedule through to planning a wedding or party, you follow a series of sequential thoughts to arrive at a solution. The faculty of reason allows you to organize these thoughts into logical steps.

It's easy to be logical when there are no other pressures, but in real life, decisions often need to be made quickly when you are stressed and under pressure. Filtering out these emotional factors will help you make more objective decisions with greater authority, both at work and at home.

TEST YOUR RESPONSE

After dinner with friends, you come back alone to find a deserted parking lot and your car with its tires slashed, the windows broken, and the stereo stolen. How would you feel if you were really in this situation? Rank these tasks in the order of your plan of action:

A. Call a tow truck.

B. Inform your insurance company of what has happened.

C. Prepare an inventory of the things that have been stolen.

D. Go back to the restaurant and seek some assistance.

E. Phone the police to report the incident.

F. Call a taxi to go home.

G. Remove any remaining valuables from your car.

ANSWERS & INTERPRETATIONS

Your first priority should be to protect yourself; you shouldn't tackle this on your own [D].

Your second priority should be to safeguard your property, so return to the car with someone you know and trust to draw up an inventory to claim insurance [C] and take any valuables away with you [G].

Arrange for a taxi to take you home [F], where you can begin to search for any relevant paperwork and documents.

Your third priority should be to sort things out. Contact police headquarters and report your loss, giving your name, license plate, and location [E].

Call your insurance company to fill them in on what has happened [B].

Make arrangements for your car to be removed from the scene of the crime and taken to a mechanic for immediate repair [A].

EXCELLENT

If your task order was D–C–G–F–E–B–A or similar, you have excellent logical reasoning, even under emotional pressure. You are able to use effective problem-solving strategies like working backward and breaking a problem down into smaller, more manageable parts. You would shine in an environment where logic and keeping a cool head are of importance. You have good leadership skills, which could be applied to both your working or personal life.

AVERAGE

If you considered the practicalities and thought each task through, but found it difficult to prioritize and rationalize your thought processes, you have average logical reasoning and the test's emotive nature proved a bit distracting. You might succeed in a career where emotions and logic work in harmony.

Boosting tips

1. Imagine that you want to redecorate a room. List the order of work you would undertake and say why. For example, what would you paint first—walls or ceiling, and at what point would you put in the new floor covering?

2. Buy a ready-to-assemble kit and try to work out the order in which you would put separate parts or pieces together *before* reading the instructions. Then look back at the manual to see how accurate your visual predictions were.

Can you see patterns and sequences?

SCHOOLS AND BUSINESSES often assess potential candidates' logical reasoning as part of their selection processes. These tests use visual prompts to guide subjects through specific patterns and sequences. Many real-life situations employ recognizable symbols. If you hire or buy a car, for example, it is likely that you'll be able to second-guess how to operate the dashboard controls (like turning on the air conditioning) without having to read through the manual first. You know that the signifier for this is a snowflake or that blue and red usually denote hot and cold respectively, because you learn to recognize the pattern in these symbols from other contexts like your faucets. Noticing similarities and transferring existing knowledge is evidence of logical thinking.

The ability to think logically is a great asset in stressful or recurring situations, or as part of problem-solving. Imagine you come home from work to find the kitchen flooded. You would initially try to establish the potential cause of a leak, then rationalize what course of action to take. Did you leave the dishwasher or the faucets running? Did a drainpipe burst? Working through a sequence of decisions compels you to look for patterns to solve a problem.

TEST YOUR ABILITY

1 *Which arrow is next in the sequence?*

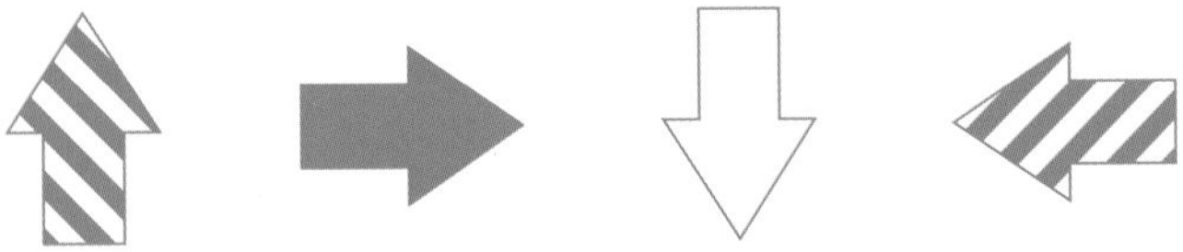

A B C

2 *Which clockface belongs with the others?*

A B C

3 *Which is the missing symbol?*

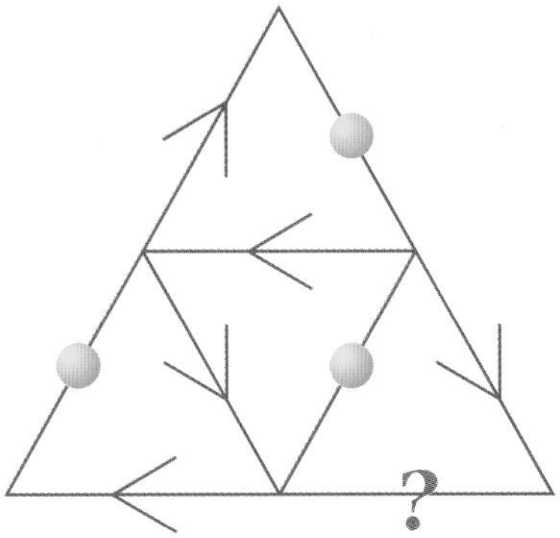

A B C

4 *If you press ALT + A on the keyboard, BC appears on the screen. What appears if you press ALT + 1?*

A 12 B 2 C 23

5 *Which one would complete your hand at cards?*

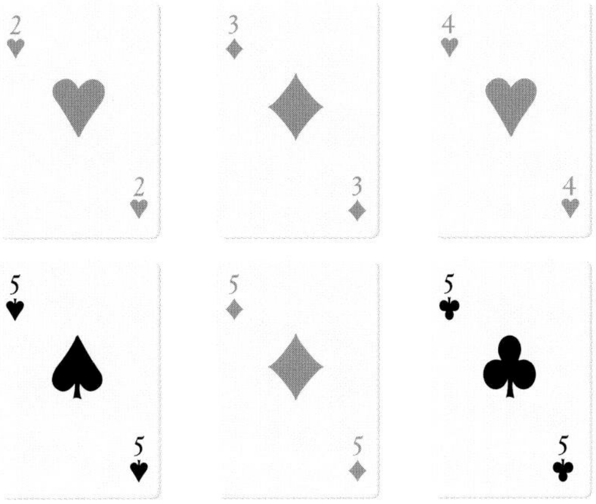

A B C

Boosting tips

1. Cut a cartoon strip from a newspaper or magazine into its individual frames, scramble them up, and arrange them in a logical sequence.

2. Create sequences and patterns with words. Write down a two-letter word like "as" or "to" and keep adding a letter each time to make a new word. For example, "at," "eat," "tame," "meats," "stream," and "streams."

3. Find a pattern you can see—stripes, for example—on your clothing, in your home, or outside your window. Write down five key features. Is it straight or wavy, horizontal or vertical? What colors does it contain? Is it geometric?

ANSWERS & INTERPRETATIONS

Score 1 point for each correct answer Maximum score = 5

1. C
2. A
3. A
4. C
5. B

3 points or less—you have average logical reasoning, enjoy creative tasks, and probably see logical thinking as mental strait-jacketing. Enhance rigorous thinking by trying to develop one fully formed idea to its conclusion.

4 points or more—you have excellent logical reasoning, discriminate between relevant and irrelevant information, sequence visual material, and excel at planning or project management tasks like moving or organizing a party.

Are you left- or right-brained?

LOGICAL THINKING involves two problem-solving styles which individually reflect the way the brain's adjacent hemispheres work: the left side concentrates on detail and analysis, the right side specializes in lateral and creative thinking. Both hemispheres are linked, but one side usually dominates an individual's way of thinking at any given time.

Most occupations require a balance or combination of thinking styles. The legal profession is a perfect example of this process in action—when preparing a court case, a lawyer must be predominantly left-brained in his or her analysis of a client's case and in systematically collecting the necessary material to successfully argue it without overlooking or dismissing any facts that could be used by the opposition. He or she will then have to draw upon right-brain processes to respond to new evidence and unexpected testimonies throughout the trial, and to creatively argue the client's position before the judge and jury while keeping focused on the essence of the chosen argument. During a court case, the jury must apply a combination of thinking styles: keeping an open mind throughout while listening to the evidence at every hearing, and logical thinking and reasoning to finally reach a verdict.

WHAT'S YOUR ANSWER?

Choose the answers that best describe you.

1. When I get dressed in the morning:
a) I go for the fresh clothes I have carefully laid out the night before.
b) What I choose to wear depends on the mood I'm in when I wake up or on what I find lying around that's clean.

2. If I go out with friends:
a) I like to go to a familiar place where I usually have a good time.
b) I prefer to try out new places where I've never been before.

3. At work, my desk is:
a) Tidy, with everything neatly filed and organized.
b) Covered with papers so that everything is immediately to hand if I need it.

4. On Fridays:
a) I like to have my weekend already planned so I have things to look forward to.
b) I like to leave my weekend free and spontaneous.

5. My hobbies could be described as:
a) Requiring focus, research, and analysis.
b) Requiring creativity, imagination, and spontaneity.

Boosting tips

1. If you are left-brained, put together a "mood book." Collect different pictures and objects that appeal to you: a feather, a leaf, a magazine cutout. Paste them into your scrapbook and review your collection. How does it make you feel? Making an emotional—not a logical—connection between objects helps develop right-brain thinking.

2. If you are right-brained, look at a newspaper. Close your eyes. Put your finger on a word on the page. Write it down. Repeat this process until you have 10 words. Make up a short story around these words exactly as they are written. Using words that you haven't freely chosen helps develop left-brain thinking.

ANSWERS & INTERPRETATIONS

Mostly a's—you have a tendency toward left-brain activity and solve problems by relying on information and facts before reaching a decision. Your major drawbacks are a resistance to new ideas and the potential suppression of creativity by evaluating ideas before they are fully formed.

Mostly b's—you have a tendency toward right-brain activity and solve problems creatively and flexibly to come up with lots of solutions. Your main disadvantage is getting bored with detail and wanting to rush on to the next challenge without having resolved previous issues.

An equal mix of a's and b's—you display centered-brain activity, with both sides working in equilibrium. This mental elasticity enables you to comfortably apply either an analytical or a creative approach. You may, however, not be either systematic or imaginative enough, which could undermine your depth of understanding or limit your ability to switch between left- and right-brain decisions.

THE TWO HEMISPHERES OF THE BRAIN (viewed from below)

The right hemisphere is associated with spatial construction, non-verbal creativity, and visual processing, but has no specialist regions.

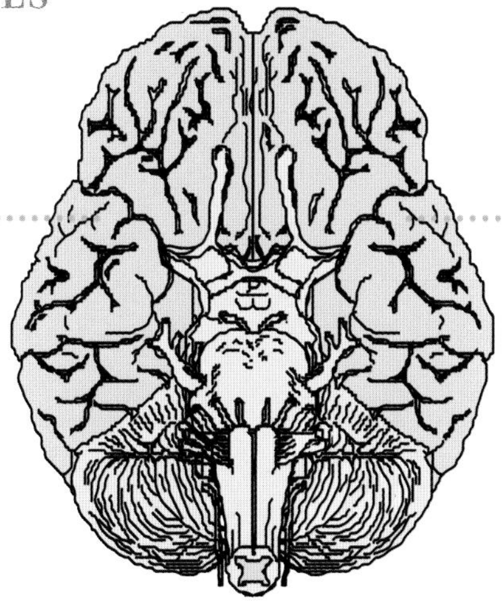

The left hemisphere is associated with linguistic function, speech production, the ability to write and understand written words, and plays a crucial role in mathematical calculation and logical deduction.

Can you visualize in two dimensions?

Spatial reasoning allows us to make sense of our moving and changing world. It calls on the ability to mentally manipulate two-dimensional objects, and to recognize an object or shape when viewing it from different angles. Graphic designers use this skill when creating books or magazines; so do pattern cutters in fashion and textile design when translating garment sketches into paper patterns. Spatial reasoning in two dimensions is needed for reading a road or a subway map, because the orientation of the map is often different to the direction in which you want to travel. Being able to accurately rotate the map in your head will help you reach your destination more quickly and efficiently.

TEST YOUR ABILITY

1 *Which of these shapes is not present in this picture?*

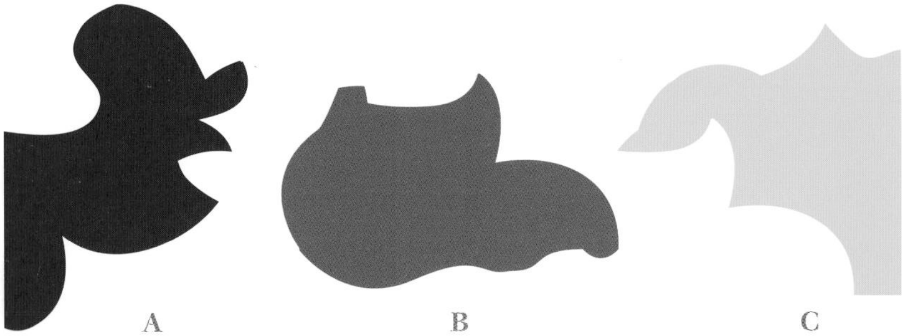

A B C

2 *Which is the next shape in the sequence?*

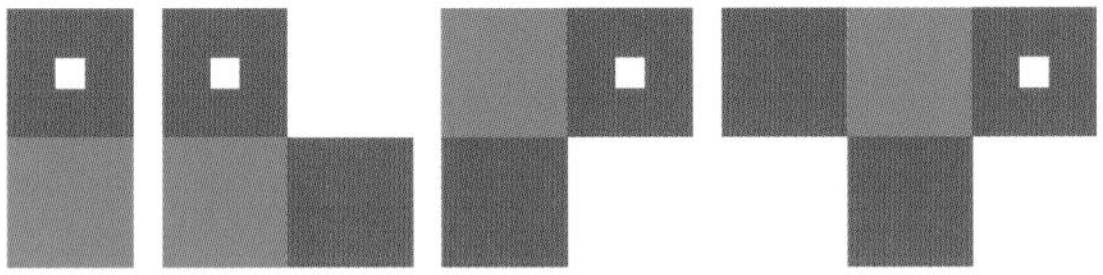

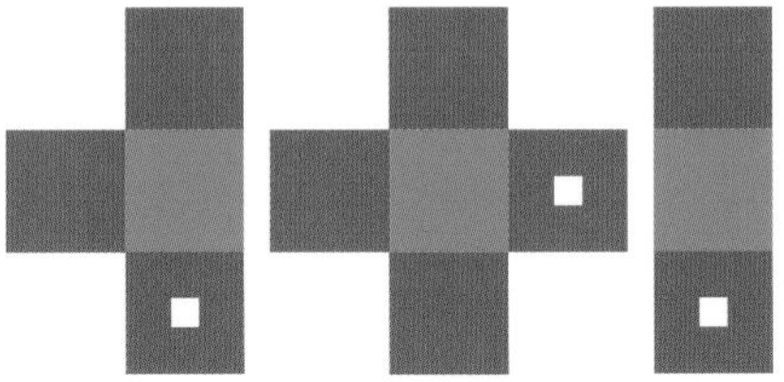

A B C

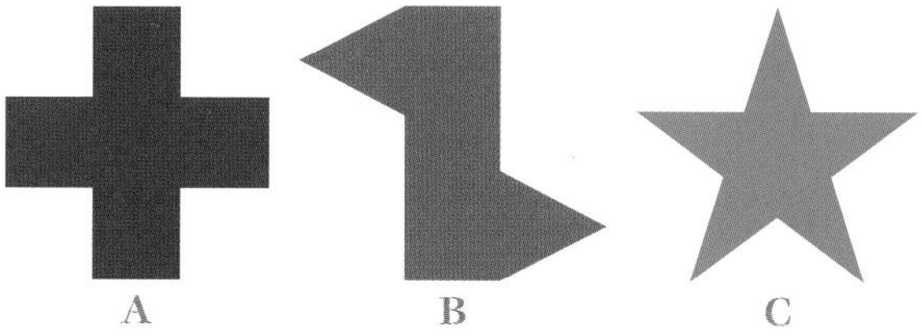

3 *Which of these shapes is the odd one out?*

4 *How many different squares can you see in this grid?*

A 9

B 10

C 14

5 *Which of these shapes is not the same?*

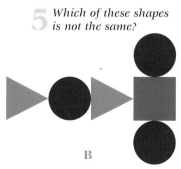

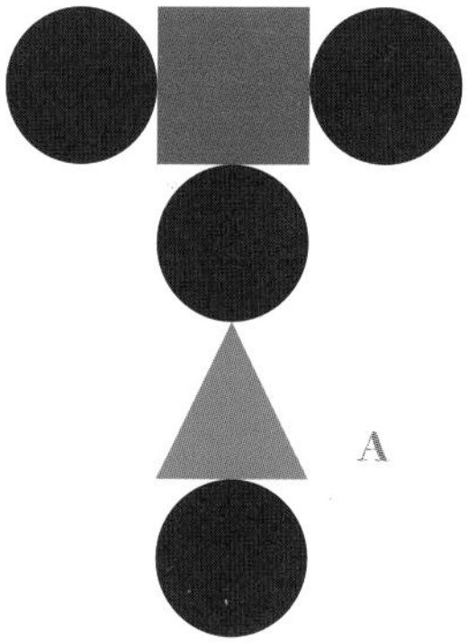

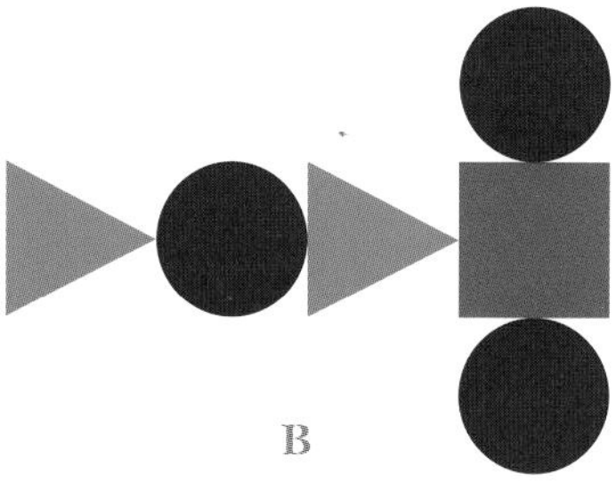

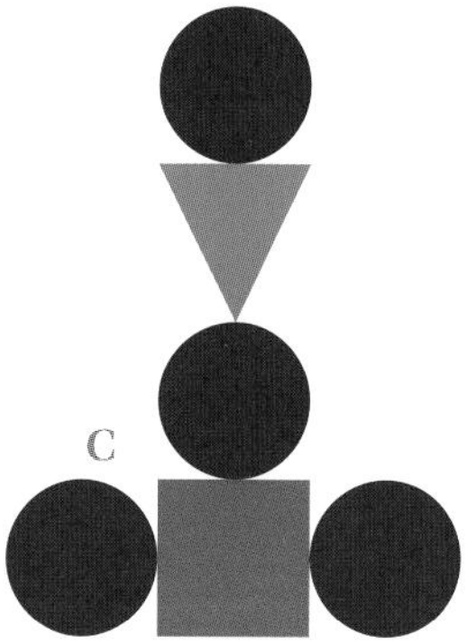

ANSWERS & INTERPRETATIONS

Score 1 point for each correct answer
Maximum score = 5

1. B
2. A
3. B
4. C
5. B

3 points or less—you have average spatial reasoning, and probably found these tasks a little challenging. To improve, try reading words that are upside down by imagining the letters the right way up using mental orientation.

4 points or more—you have excellent spatial reasoning, and probably enjoy using your sight the most out of all your senses. Try to develop your talent further through a visual hobby such as photography.

Boosting tips

1. With a pencil and paper, sit at one end of a room and sketch the layout. Then do the same at the other end so that you have sketches of the layout from both perspectives.

2. When you next walk or drive to somewhere that's unfamiliar, use a map instead of asking for directions or taking the long way on familiar roads.

3. Create your own jigsaw puzzle. Draw an image of your choice, color it in, cut it up into several pieces (no less than 10), scramble them up, and reassemble it.

Can you visualize in three dimensions?

FROM INTERACTIVE software to driving on the highway, the demands on our visuo-spatial abilities are changing and becoming ever more challenging. Three-dimensional spatial reasoning involves visualizing an object, mentally manipulating it in space, and picturing the outcome. Architecture is a profession which requires this skill: draftspeople will have three-dimensional versions of buildings, as seen from different angles, in their heads before sitting down to sketch two-dimensional plans at the design stage of projects. Video game designers likewise possess three-dimensional representations of the worlds contained within the games they are developing. They can mold and bend these to produce continuously new and entertaining scenarios and outcomes for players.

This type of reasoning is used by most of us when three-dimensional and two-dimensional objects intersect with one another in daily life. It could come in handy when finding your way around a shopping mall, when trying to reach an empty space that you've spied across the parking lot, or negotiating your way around an unfamiliar office floor.

TEST YOUR ABILITY

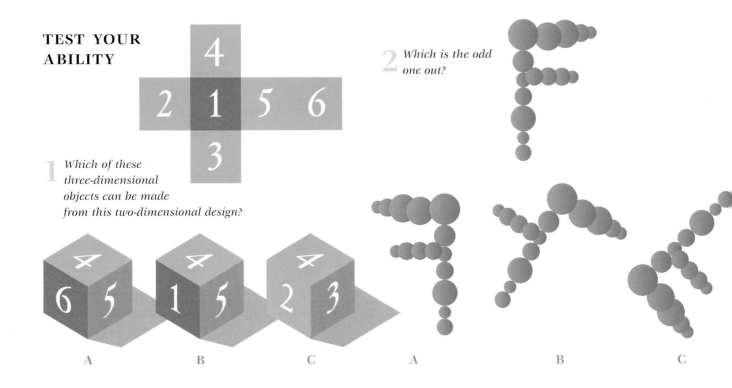

1 *Which of these three-dimensional objects can be made from this two-dimensional design?*

A B C

2 *Which is the odd one out?*

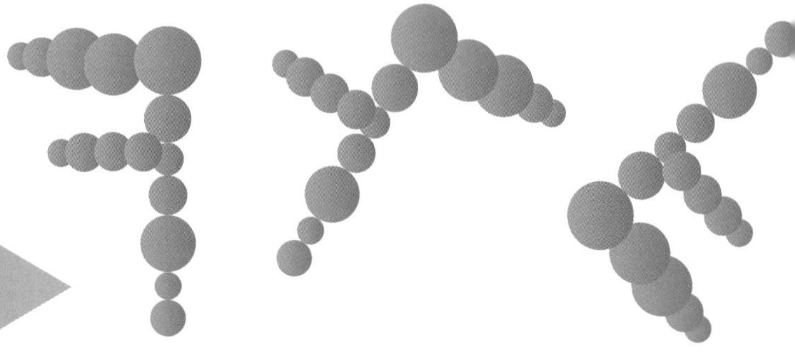

A B C

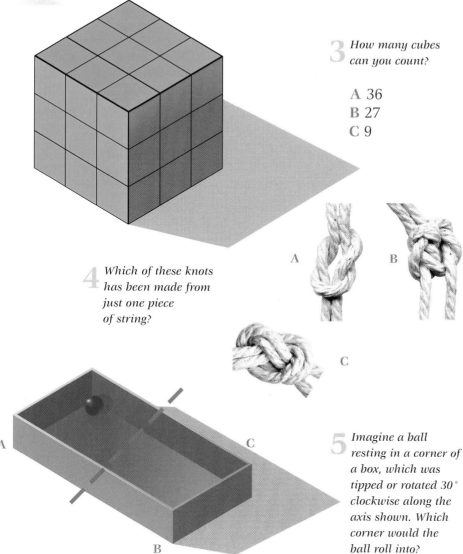

3 *How many cubes can you count?*

A 36
B 27
C 9

4 *Which of these knots has been made from just one piece of string?*

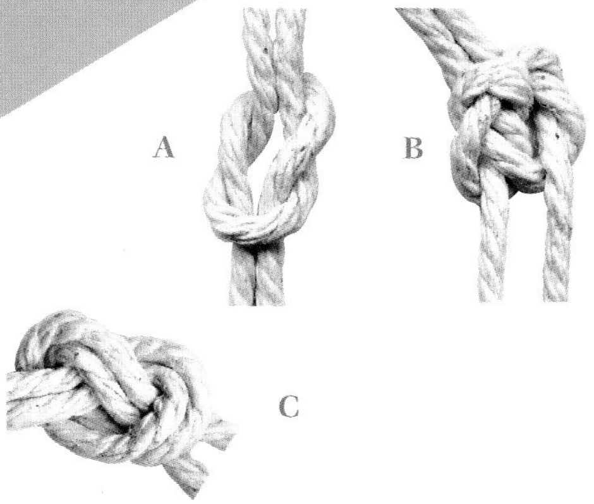

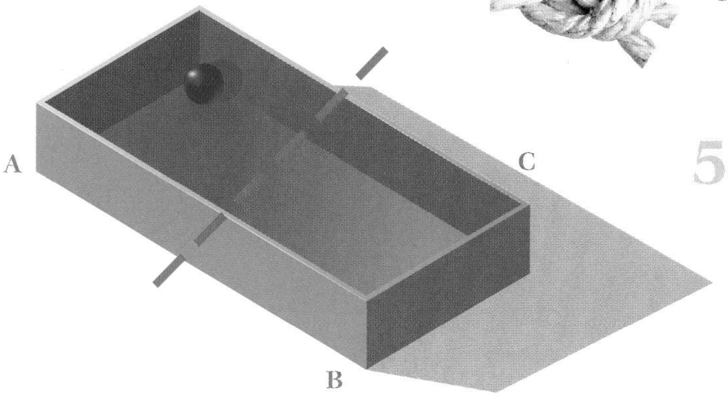

5 *Imagine a ball resting in a corner of a box, which was tipped or rotated 30° clockwise along the axis shown. Which corner would the ball roll into?*

Boosting tips

1. Build a box out of a flat piece of cardboard. Then make an envelope from a piece of paper.

2. Imagine your route into work exactly as you walk or drive it every morning and evening. Picture every corner you turn, every landmark you pass, every door you walk through.

ANSWERS & INTERPRETATIONS

Score 1 point for each correct answer Maximum score = 5

1. B
2. B
3. A
4. C
5. C

3 points or less—you have average three-dimensional spatial reasoning, can orientate yourself reasonably well, and provide reliable directions when this is required. You probably find it easiest to mentally manipulate an object if it's in front of you.

4 points or more—you have excellent three-dimensional spatial reasoning, and can visualize and manipulate objects from various angles in your head. You can create 3-D objects in your imagination.

Can you transform dimensions?

THE ULTIMATE method of testing spatial reasoning centers around transforming two-dimensional plans into actual three-dimensional objects, and being able to deconstruct three-dimensional objects back into their two-dimensional outlines. Improving on this skill could literally transform your life: assembling flat-pack furniture or setting up kitchen units will be a cinch, installing your own fax machine a snap. These types of mundane tasks involve interpreting two-dimensional instructions to create or operate three-dimensional objects.

Nowadays many occupations, particularly those with a strong design element, depend on an ability to transform objects across dimensions. Fashion designers create patterns on cloth from drawings to bring to life three-dimensional mental images of creations. Urban planners alternate between two-dimensional street map layouts and three-dimensional mental plans for cityscapes with consummate ease and skill. Air traffic controllers reason spatially across dimensions since the moving dots on their screens represent the trajectory of real planes, which have to be managed with great care to ensure the air safety of passengers and crew.

TEST YOUR ABILITY

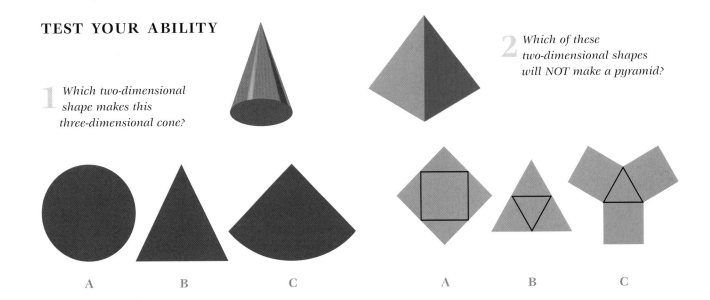

1 *Which two-dimensional shape makes this three-dimensional cone?*

A B C

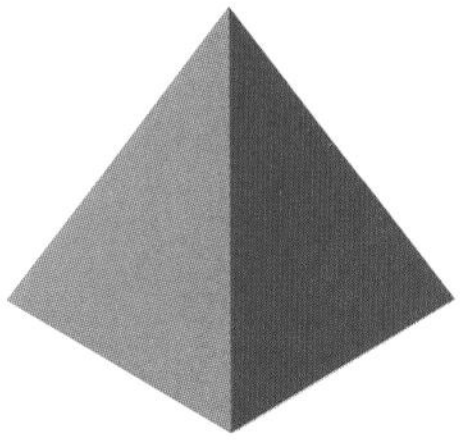

2 *Which of these two-dimensional shapes will NOT make a pyramid?*

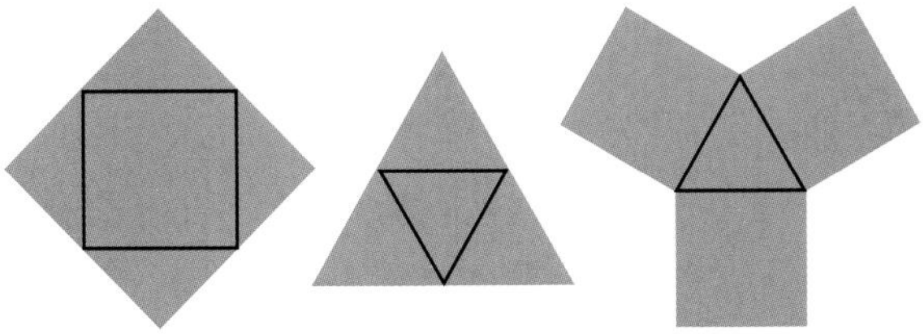

A B C

3 *Which order would these strips need to be in to construct this beach ball?*

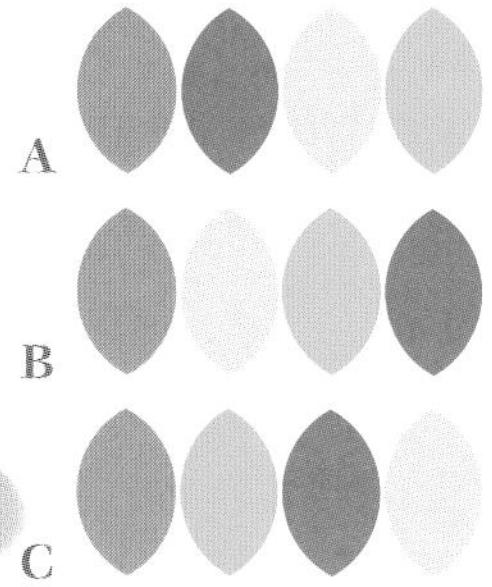

4 *Which shape could be made from these sets of instructions?*

Fix A at right angles to B.
Then fix C at right angles to D.
Then fix A at right angles to C.

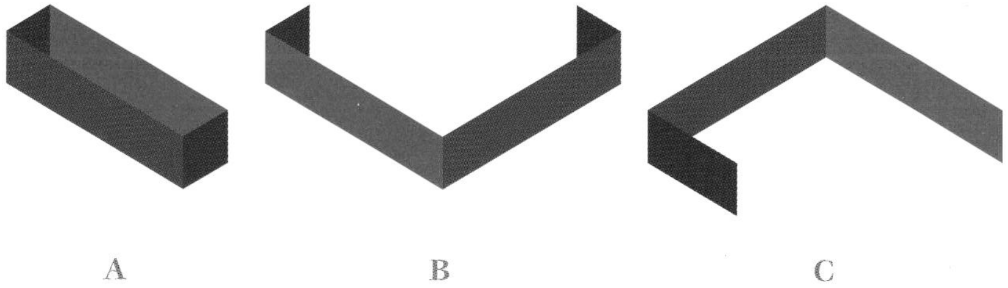

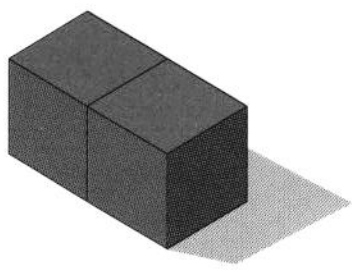

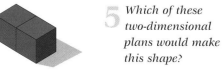

5 *Which of these two-dimensional plans would make this shape?*

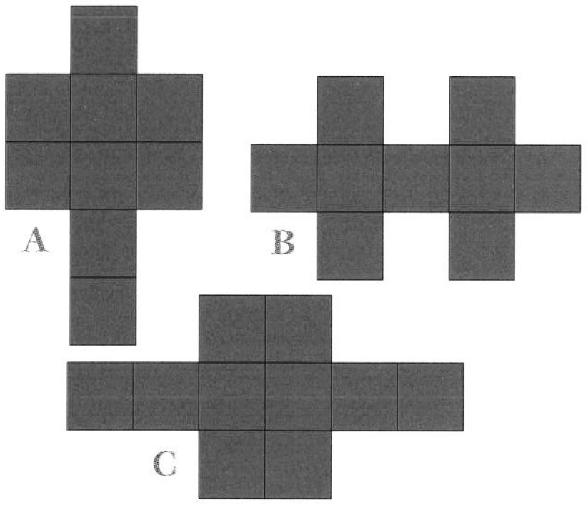

Boosting tips

1. Before making furniture or toys, read the instructions. Lay all the component parts in front of you. Notice how two-dimensional diagrams in the plans translate into three-dimensional objects.
2. Using a piece of paper, scissors, and scotch tape, construct a cone. Then try making a cube.
3. Flatten an empty tissue box into its two-dimensional shape. Is it what you expected?

ANSWERS & INTERPRETATIONS

Score 1 point for each correct answer
Maximum score = 5

1. C
2. C
3. A
4. B
5. C

3 points or less—you have average two- to three-dimensional spatial reasoning. Boosting this skill would enable you to approach locations or reach destinations from different directions without getting lost, making you more spatially aware of the world around you.

4 points or more—you have excellent two- to three-dimensional spatial reasoning, and are able to mentally transform images into 3-D objects. You find it easy to visualize, design, and make objects.

Are you a decoder?

WIDELY ACCEPTED as one of the fairest assessment methods in existence, abstract reasoning is measured by questions that do not rely on previous knowledge, experience, or cultural specificity. This makes for "purer" testing methods—there is no knowledge advantage or bias in the content of the question. Questionnaires involving decoding (or spotting a pattern) are the traditional abstract reasoning test format used by schools and businesses.

There are everyday advantages to be had from exercising good abstract reasoning other than gaining admission to schools and excelling at job interviews. If you are asked to join a specialist project where everyone is using jargon, you will be able to quickly decode this new vocabulary. Filling in boxes on forms with abbreviated headings will also prove easy. On your next vacation in a foreign country where you don't speak the language, try relying on your abstract reasoning skills to correctly decipher and interpret the meaning of unfamiliar signs, symbols, and words.

TEST YOUR ABILITY

1

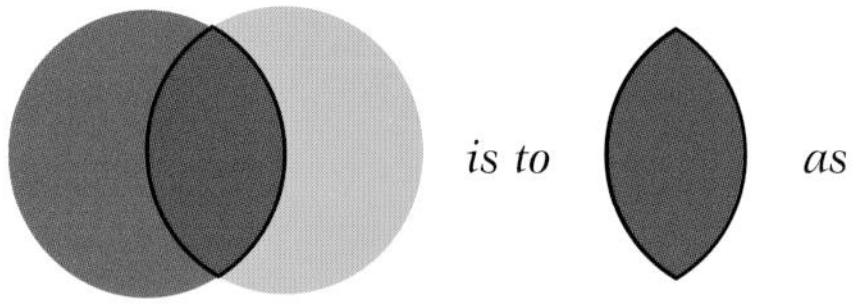

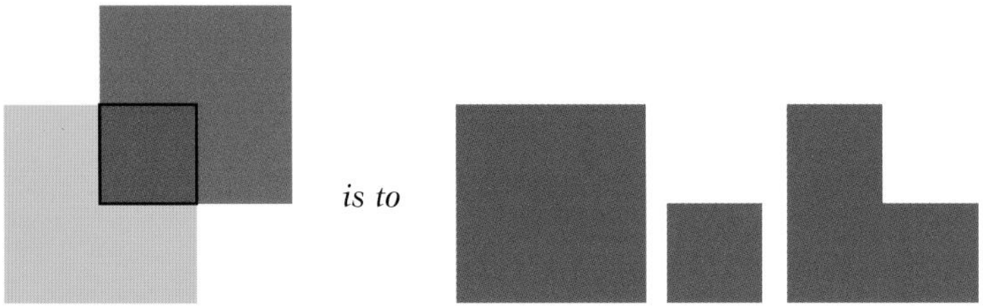

A B C

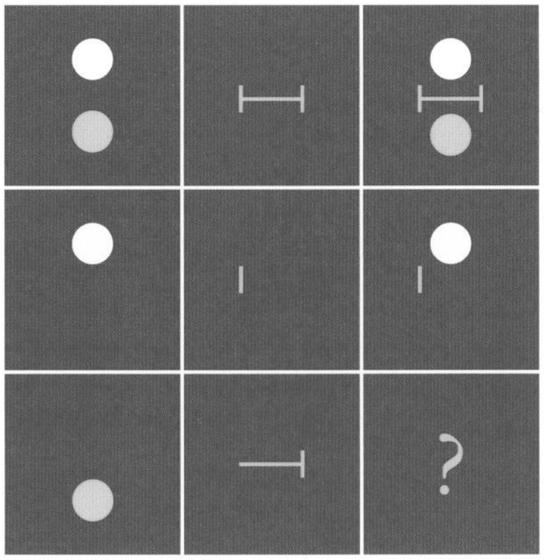

2 *Look along each line and down each column. Which symbol belongs in the empty square?*

A B C

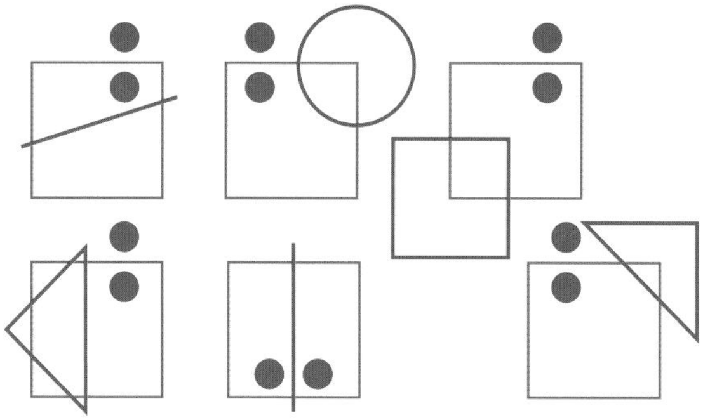

A B C

3 *What is the fourth shape belonging to the top set?*

4 *Which of the circles on the right is most like the one on the left?*

A B C

5 *Which column is the odd one out?*

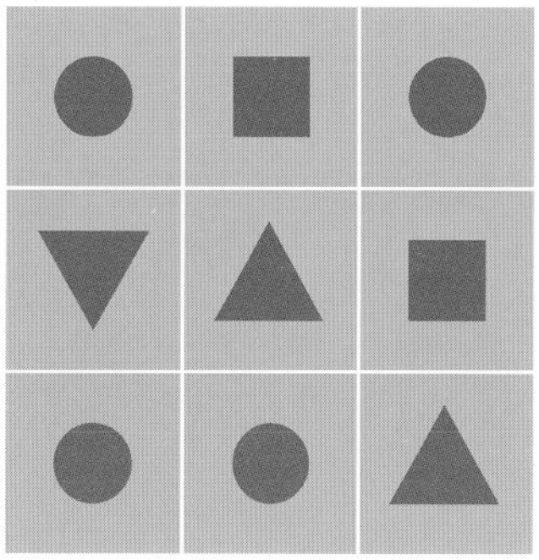

A B C

Boosting tips

1. Draw a floor plan of your office. Invent symbols for features like bathrooms, meeting rooms, fire exits, and stairwells. Test your key on a colleague and get him or her to work out what each sign on your plan represents.

2. Play a game with friends based around guessing a secret code. Get the other players to ask you questions, to which you answer using your chosen code like leaving out words with the letter "t," or answering every question starting with the letter "i." The first person to guess the code wins. Take it in turns to invent a code and answer questions.

ANSWERS & INTERPRETATIONS

Score 1 point for each correct answer
Maximum score = 5

1. B
2. A
3. C
4. A
5. A

3 points or less—you have average abstract reasoning, and can interpret familiar codes through clearly set out rules like traffic signs, but might struggle with complex codes in unconventional contexts like computer programming.

4 points or more—you have excellent abstract reasoning, and can manipulate and decipher information by establishing codes, useful in learning or speaking another language.

Could you find your way out of a maze?

MAZES ARE PUZZLES characterized by a single correct route and many branching paths designed to distract. The labyrinth, one of the oldest maze forms, has only one track and a central destination. Believed to symbolize the spiritual journey of pilgrims in Christianity, mazes were very popular during the Middle Ages and can still be found emblazoned on the windows and floors of cathedrals and Gothic churches throughout Europe.

Today mazes are still being used in commercially subtle ways. In retail design, department stores have floors which are shrewdly arranged with a predetermined consumer journey in mind: a twisting path is laid down for the shopper to follow with branches to distract from, and delay arrival at, the final destination. For example, customers searching for popular items such as underwear and perfume will, say, be "coerced" into walking past leather goods and accessories (all on the same level) to reach the other departments, deliberately located at the back. In contrast with department stores, supermarkets are laid out like labyrinths with a set path marking out separate sections, all of which lead to a check-out counter. In this way, supermarket chains ensure that walking down every aisle represents a potential purchasing "journey" for their customers.

TEST YOUR ABILITY

Cover the answers on the opposite page. Place a piece of tracing paper over each maze or use a light pencil and see if you can find your way out.

Maze 1

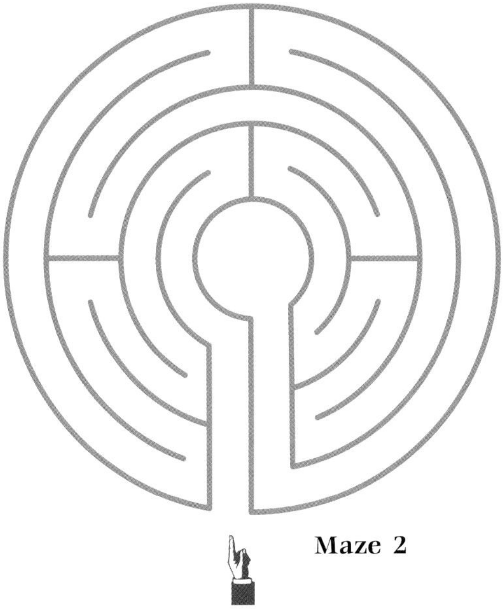

Maze 2

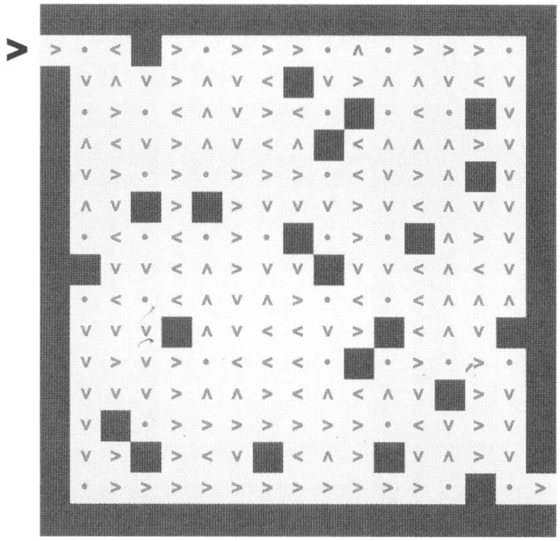

Maze 3

Follow the arrowheads, but note that you can only change direction on a dot.

Boosting tips

1. Design your own maze. Using a sheet of graph or grid paper, trace a 15 x 15 box (225 squares in total). Mark the entry and exit points on it. Use the grid and a pencil to sketch the route and dead end paths. Add the walls in pen and erase the pencil lines. Try it out on a friend.

2. Observe the layout of your living or office space. Notice how the position of items of furniture dictates the route that you walk to and from key areas. Are there any dead ends (as in a maze), or circular routes (as in a labyrinth)?

ANSWERS & INTERPRETATIONS

Maze 1

Maze 2

AVERAGE

If you found mazes 1 and 2 difficult to negotiate, particularly if you took several wrong turnings, you have average abstract reasoning.

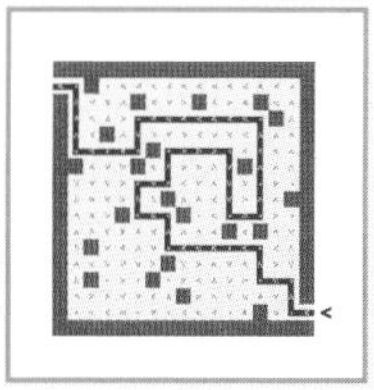

Maze 3

EXCELLENT

If you completed mazes 1, 2, and 3 successfully with few, if any, errors, you have excellent abstract reasoning. Your ability to foresee obstacles and test different answer options is a great problem-solving technique, useful at home and at work.

Can you sort things out?

Abstract reasoning involves decoding and seeing patterns in symbols and shapes. When this skill is applied to daily living as a cataloging system, it can create or restore order where chaos rules. Tidying up your life reduces stress levels and creates more free time—you'll know where to look for things and be able to prioritize what needs to be done, in what order, and by when.

Both the private and public sectors use classification systems to make things easier to access and track. Music shops use an alphabetical ordering system by artist name to file stock; government offices may use social security numbers. Proper filing ensures vital data is always to hand and doesn't go missing.

TEST YOUR ABILITY

Imagine that you supply a custom tailoring service with three types of buttons. These have three different levels of usage and are sewn on to three types of garment—shirts, pants, and coats.

high-level usage
(they are repeatedly done and undone during the day)

medium-level usage
(once they are done up in the morning, they are unlikely to be used again before undressing)

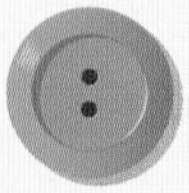

low-level usage
(they are rarely done or undone and are mostly for decoration)

You also know that:

- shirts have buttons on the cuffs and down the front for fastening
- pants have buttons on the waistband and on the back pockets
- coats have decorative buttons on the sleeves and front-fastening buttons

What are the criteria you would use to organize your button samples into categories (i.e. number of holes on the button)?

Boosting tips

1. Create patterns and order in your personal life: choose an area you feel is chaotic such as your make-up bag or tool kit. Plan the way you want to retrieve things in future, and organize your storage system on this basis.
2. Overhaul your filing system at work by creating categories under which to file given documents. Test this on a colleague to see whether information is accessed more quickly and efficiently.
3. Sort your monthly bills into categories: food, housing, entertainment, clothes, transport, and miscellaneous. This will facilitate adding up the total expenditure at the end of the month per group in order to compare costs.

ANSWERS & INTERPRETATIONS

There are no right or wrong answers. Score 1 point if you organized the buttons by each of the following categories:

1. level of usage
2. number of holes
3. position on the garment
4. garment type
5. number of buttons per garment

3 points or less—you have average abstract reasoning. You find it easier to use existing codes and patterns rather than creating your own.

4 points or more—you have excellent abstract reasoning, enjoy looking for similarities and ways of classifying things, and probably are well-organized in your approach to life.

Your conceptual intelligence

NOW THAT YOU'VE completed all the tests, you can profile your results to get an overall view of your strengths. Check the relevant boxes for each of your test scores.

Are you predominantly left-, center-, or right-brained?

From the logical reasoning test (*see pages 20-21*), note whether you displayed an overall preference for left-, center-, or right-brain thinking processes.

- If you have 5 or more checks in the average column, you have adequate conceptual intelligence. You are likely to be right-brained by nature and take a holistic approach to life. You prefer to learn by having a general overview of a topic first, and then go on to explore the specifics.

	Average ✓	*Excellent* ✓
LOGICAL REASONING		
***Test 1* (pages 16-17)**		
***Test 2* (pages 18-19)**		
SPATIAL REASONING		
***Test 1* (pages 22-23)**		
***Test 2* (pages 24-25)**		
***Test 3* (pages 26-27)**		
ABSTRACT REASONING		
***Test 1* (pages 28-29)**		
***Test 2* (pages 30-31)**		
***Test 3* (pages 32-33)**		

- If you have 3-4 checks in either column, you have good conceptual intelligence. You are likely to be center-brained by nature and feel comfortable looking at the whole picture as well as the detail. You probably take a global approach in some areas of your life, and are systematic in others.
- If you have 5 or more checks in the excellent column, you have superior conceptual intelligence. You are likely to left-brained by nature and are analytical in your approach. You prefer to learn in a step-by-step sequence, beginning with the details and gradually arriving at an overall understanding.

Developing and improving conceptual intelligence

Traditionally viewed as the raw, core intelligence that you are genetically hardwired with from birth, there are a variety of ways of developing conceptual intelligence and improving test scores. One of the most important influencing factors is drive, although it is essential to remember that increased motivation levels tend to maximize your performance rather than actually raise it.

If you possess adequate-to-good conceptual intelligence, set yourself significant but realistic targets. Learn to narrow down your focus and apply logic to a given situation. Methodically work your way through the reasons why you want and deserve something like a raise, for example, and discard any emotional justifications you may have that might interfere with your logical reasoning.

If you have superior conceptual intelligence, practice adapting your strategies to suit different contexts. Knowledge of this talent may have come as a pleasant surprise. Conceptual intelligence is a metacognitive skill, which means you have to consciously consider the mechanics behind the way you think in order to achieve insight. You need to learn to control cognition as you would physical body movement: your brain, like your body, can be trained and developed through regular workouts. Volunteer to find a solution to a project problem at work, or find unusual ways of making your life easier at home.

Working with children

Here are some fun projects for youngsters to develop and improve their conceptual intelligence in conjunction with your own. You could, for instance:

- Build three-dimensional constructions from blocks or Lego pieces. Challenge the child to build something extraordinary such as a skyscraper or a spaceship. Observe how he or she plans and sets about the task and gently offer guidance only where it is needed.
- Create your own "secret" language: a written code that only you two (or a small group) can decipher!
- Devise a map for a treasure hunt. Older children can draw and write clues for younger children, or teams can take it in turns to make up the trail and then be the searchers.

2

information to be recalled individually. When an individual forgets a "fact," he or she has no strategy for reconstructing it. Students lose initiative and confidence to take the next step needed in order to learn more information.

As the "science of patterns," mathematics is not just about number facts. People with numerical intelligence are able to see and create patterns. Understanding both the facts and the relationships between them helps to build a solid foundation of information and strategies. Mathematical skill and confidence grow by being able to link new problems to existing knowledge. Mental arithmetic is the first basic step to understanding math facts. Once these are in place, numerical reasoning can develop.

Mental arithmetic

Numerical intelligence is based on different quantities being represented by distinct digits, and numbers being "acted upon" by the mathematical functions of addition, subtraction, multiplication, and division. The ability to mentally undertake these operations without the use of a calculator is called mental arithmetic—a prerequisite for more complicated computations and manipulations.

Mental arithmetic can be initially developed using pen and paper, or beads (such as an abacus). The brain can be trained to imagine writing numbers down or using beads, so that calculations are ultimately done entirely in the mind.

Numerical reasoning

Although mental arithmetic is part of numerical intelligence, being able to reason with numbers presents more opportunities than would simple straightforward mental calculation. Numerical reasoning takes numbers from the realm of theory into that of practice and requires both creative and logical thinking. Core reasoning skills, involving data assessment, calculation proposals, and solutions, need to be applied.

Why is numerical intelligence important?

Numbers play a major part in daily living. They assist us in making sense of our immediate environments and enable us to quantify, plan ahead, predict, and discover. All jobs have a numerical component, and our private lives benefit from number confidence: taking out a loan, budgeting, furnishing an apartment, or even cooking. Traits of numerically inclined individuals include an enjoyment of problem-solving, measuring, sequencing, collecting data, performing mathematical calculations, and creating spreadsheets and databases. Professions that seek out individuals with excellent numerical aptitude include scientists, mathematicians, statisticians, accountants, bankers, business managers, retailers, and researchers.

Are you good at adding and subtracting?

CHILDREN DEVELOP mathematical abilities from a very young age. They begin sorting by category, then learn numbers off by heart, and eventually come to appreciate that a single number is related to a single object—true counting has begun.

The foundation skills of mental arithmetic are addition and subtraction: with these firmly in place, the world of mathematics begins to unfold. As part of your daily routine, mental arithmetic is essential to checking that you've been given the correct change in a store, calculating how much time you have left before your next appointment, feeding a parking meter, working out the distance you've covered jogging through the park, and many other tasks. It is also essential for keeping tabs on your expenditure so you don't have any nasty surprises at the end of the month.

TEST YOUR SKILLS

You will need a pen and paper and a stopwatch or a clock with a second hand. Time yourself on the speed and accuracy of your answers.

1 *What is the total value of these playing cards?*

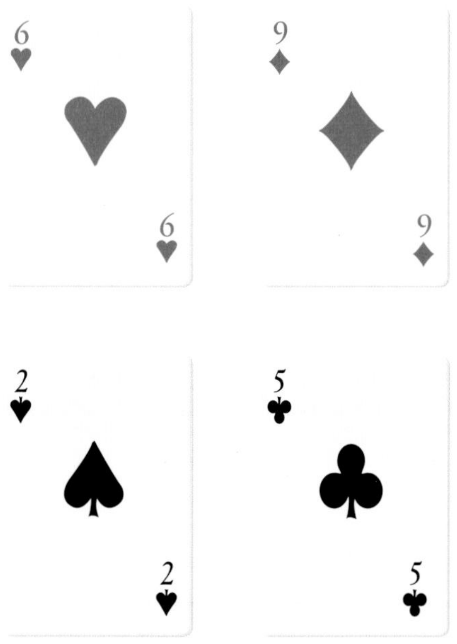

2 *Which is larger—the sum of the top numbers on these dominoes, or the sum of their bottom numbers?*

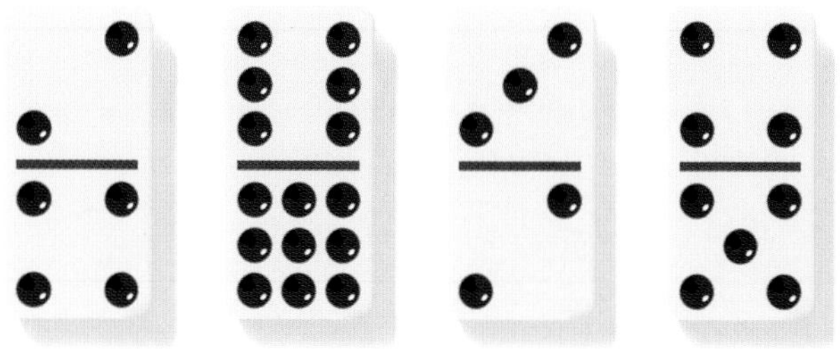

3 *What is the sum of the visible faces on these dice?*

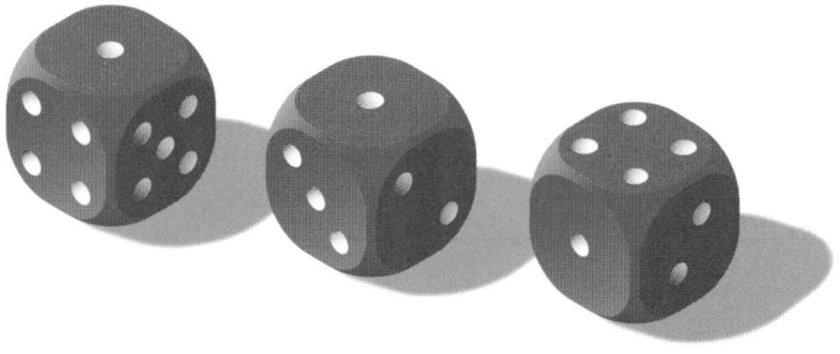

4 *You need 12 nails to build a storage box. How many spares would you have if you bought a pack of 25?*

5 *You buy 3 packs of gum for 50 cents each. How much change would you get from a $5 bill?*

6 *The thermometer records 75° during the day with temperatures dropping by 28° in the evening. What is the reading at night-time?*

7 *You're watching a movie that is 122 minutes long. After an hour, you sneak out into the foyer for a couple of minutes to buy more popcorn. How much of the movie is there left to run?*

ANSWERS & INTERPRETATIONS

Score 1 point for each correct answer
Maximum score = 7

1. 22
2. bottom
3. 23
4. 13
5. $3.50
6. 47°
7. 60 minutes

Under 75 seconds and no incorrect answers—you have excellent addition and subtraction skills, and probably use this skill every day, whether it's checking your change, paying off what you owe, or managing your time.

Over 75 seconds or any incorrect answers—you have average addition and subtraction skills, and probably avoid using math where you can. This may be limiting to your life: good mental arithmetic will enhance your job and your personal life.

Boosting tips

1. When you think about numbers, break them down into smaller digits. If you think in units of 10, for example, try memorizing pairs of numbers that make up 10 like 3 and 7, 6 and 4.

2. Set yourself some daily tasks: add up the change in your pocket; subtract the cost of your journey to and from work; calculate how much time you spend on breaks from your working hours.

3. Estimate the cost of meals in restaurants or the goods in your trolley before the check or bill arrives.

4. Construct a timetable for cooking a meal or an evening out based on what time you want to start, when you will finish, and how long individual tasks or parts of the evening take. Add or subtract timings to arrive at your schedule.

Do you have a talent for multiplication?

MULTIPLICATION is simply a shortcut to addition. Why add 6 + 6 + 6 + 6 + 6 when you know that 6 x 5 is 30? You may feel that multiplication was something you only needed to do at school, but improving your skills will help you more quickly negotiate a wide range of tasks in real life: calculating the number of tiles needed to resurface your bathroom, pre-ordering the right amount of refreshments for party guests, or making sure you tip the correct amount for great service.

TEST YOUR SKILLS

You will need a pen and paper and a stopwatch or a clock with a second hand. Time yourself on the speed and accuracy of your answers.

1 *You're making pasta sauce for 8 guests and need 1 handful of sliced mushrooms to 1 handful of chopped onions to 2 handfuls of diced tomatoes per person. How many handfuls of tomatoes will you need in total?*

2 *How many buckets of paint do you need to buy to decorate your bedroom walls if each surface needs 2 coats and each layer uses 4 pots of paint?*

3 *You go for a jog in the park. Each circuit takes you 8 minutes. How long will it take you to complete 3 circuits?*

4 *You own 10 pairs of trainers and 6 pairs of shoes. How much footwear do you have in total?*

5 *Which is bigger?*
3 x 1 x 6   5 x 2 x 2   4 x 3 x 2

6 *You have house plants that need to be watered 3 times a week. How many times will you give them a drink during 7 weeks?*

7 *Complete this sum:*
(3 x 9) – (2 x 5) = ?

8 *There are 7 spokes on each of the 4 wheels of your car. How many spokes in total?*

9 *You are running a conference for 50 delegates, each of whom has been charged $150 when your net costs per delegate were only $50. How much profit have you made?*

10 *You have written a report for work, which is to be circulated to 8 people, 3 of whom require an extra copy. How many photocopies do you need?*

ANSWERS & INTERPRETATIONS

Score 1 point for each correct answer
Maximum score = 10

1. 16
2. 32
3. 24
4. 32
5. 4 x 3 x 2 = 24
6. 21
7. 17
8. 28
9. $5000
10. 11

Under 90 seconds and no incorrect answers—you have excellent multiplication skills. You're probably the kind of person that gets asked by your friends to calculate and convert foreign currency, and estimate interest rates on savings accounts or sales tax returns.

Over 90 seconds and any incorrect answers—you have average multiplication skills, and probably made mistakes because you were going too fast. Concentrate on being accurate. Speed comes with familiarity and practice—soon you will be able to undertake these mental calculations quickly and precisely.

Boosting tips

1. Use an actual checkerboard grid or draw your own to do this activity. With a pen, trace an 8 x 8 square grid (64 squares in total) on graph or squared paper. Write "$1" in the top left-hand square, "$2" in the square to the right of it, "$4" in the next square, then "$8," "$16," "$32," "$64," and "$128" along the first row (*see opposite*). How many dollars have you made when you reach the end of the board?

2. Start with "3" in the top left-hand square. Add 3 for the number in the following square (i.e. "6"). Keep adding 3 so that the squares read: "3," "6," "9," "12," "15," etc. Finish the calculation to complete the grid.

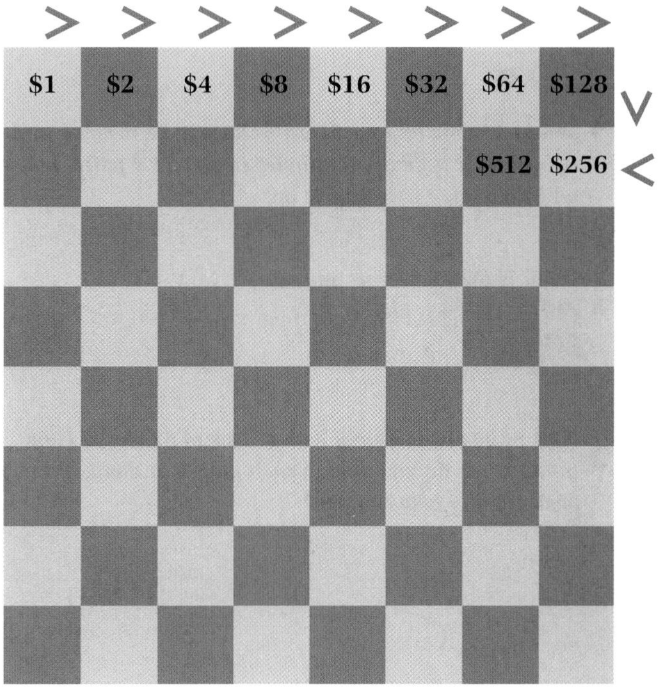

Can you play with proportions?

Fractions are a way of expressing the portion divided off in relation to the whole. The ability to use division and fractions depends on good addition, subtraction, and multiplication. If you are confident with these, you can really start to manipulate numbers. You can work out the best sale deals, go dutch on a night out, or plan the amount of new carpet or curtain fabric that you need for your bedroom.

TEST YOUR SKILLS

You will need a pen and paper and a stopwatch or a clock with a second hand. Time yourself on the speed and accuracy of your answers.

1 *You're eating out with 2 friends and the meal comes to $66, service included. How much does each one of you owe?*

2 *Which is bigger?*

1/4   2/12   4/10

3 *You take some of your favorite shoes to be re-soled and re-heeled. If it takes 30 minutes to service 4 pairs, how long does each pair take to do?*

4 *What is the answer to this sum?*
$(20 \div 5) + (18 \div 3)$

5 *Four of you are playing with a deck of 52 cards. How many cards do you deal to each player to divide the pack equally between you?*

6 *Your meal at a restaurant costs $20 and you leave a 20% tip. How much did you give the waiter?*

7 *Your company employs 50 people. You need to increase the number of employees by 30% to fulfill a new contract. How many new staff do you need to recruit?*

8 *Which of these is the odd one out?*

5/15   2/6   4/12   3/7

9 *You work on the 20th floor and the elevator breaks down. How long does it take you to get to the 15th floor if you reach the street in 12 minutes?*

10 *You've seen a leather armchair on sale, reduced by 25%. If the original price tag reads $600, how much is the discounted price?*

ANSWERS & INTERPRETATIONS

Score 1 point for each correct answer
Maximum score = 10

1. $22
2. 4/10
3. 7 minutes 30 seconds
4. 10
5. 13
6. $4
7. 15
8. 3/4
9. 3 minutes
10. $450

Under 90 seconds and no incorrect answers—you have excellent division and fraction skills, and probably get a buzz from performing fast calculations under pressure. Dividing up portions and money accurately is second nature.

Over 90 seconds or any incorrect answers—you have average division and fraction skills. You probably don't volunteer to divide up the check after a meal out with friends, but improving your math can help ensure you don't overpay!

Boosting tips

1. Take an orange. Imagine you are sharing it equally with a friend—cut it in half. What if you wanted twice as much as your friend? How many pieces would you cut it into? If there were three of you, and you only wanted a quarter, what fraction of the orange would the other two have each? Practice with other objects that you can divide, cut, and segment like a pack of cards, a loaf of bread, a cake, a bunch of grapes, or a box of staples.

2. Imagine you are visiting a shop where there's a sale on. If shoes that originally cost $70 have now been reduced by 35%, work out the reduction as a fraction of the original price. If absolute prices are shown, and a coat has been reduced to $200 from $300, what is the percentage reduction?

3. Calculate the time that you spend traveling, at work, at home awake, and sleeping as a proportion of your average day.

Can you play with numbers?

Numerical reasoning depends on the fundamentals of addition, subtraction, multiplication, and division, often used in combination. Many school subjects, particularly engineering and science, elevate this base knowledge of math into numerical reasoning.

Numerical confidence and competence are now prerequisites for the majority of jobs, and recruitment assessment batteries usually include groups of these types of tests. In your daily life, there are countless situations where you can get the most out of the numerical information that is available: getting discounts on gym membership fees, devising the best interest rates for a loan, or calculating the real cost of supplemental charges on your next dream vacation package.

TEST YOUR SKILLS

You will need a pen and paper and a stopwatch or a clock with a second hand. Time yourself on the speed and accuracy of your answers

1 *What is the missing number in the grid?*

2	3	5
5	1	6
7	4	?

2 *Assuming cats have 9 lives, a mother cat has spent 8 of hers. Some of her kittens have spent only 5 lives, others 6. Between them, the mother and her kittens have 18 lives left. How many kittens does she have?*

3 *What's the missing number in the grid?*

2	3	4	5
4	9	16	?

4 *Using only multiplication, addition, and subtraction, fill in the missing signs (x, +, or –) for the following sums in the grid:*

1	?	2	?	3	=	7
4	?	5	?	6	=	3
7	?	8	?	9	=	6

5 *A bottle of mineral water serves up to 6 glasses. How many bottles would you need to ensure that 4 people drank the same amount of water all evening long? What's the least number of glasses they would each be able to drink?*

6 *What links this number sequence?*

1 4 10 22 46

7 *A woman in a pool swims one length in 50 seconds. How long does it take her to swim her third length, if each successive one takes 20% longer than the last?*

8 *Using multiplication, division, and subtraction, how can the numbers 1, 2, 3, and 4 make 5?*

9 *John runs 3 miles in 30 minutes.*
Mary runs 4 miles in 36 minutes.
Bill runs 5 miles in 40 minutes.
Who is the fastest?

10 *You want to fill up a sandpit, and each bag contains 0.25 ft^3 of sand. How many bags would you need?*

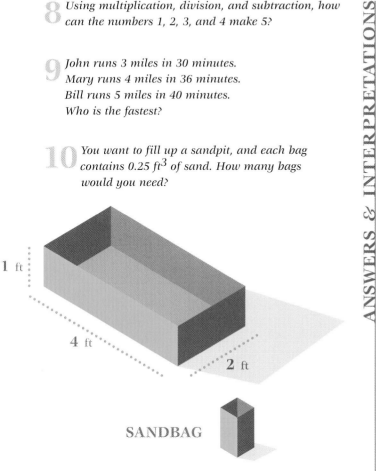

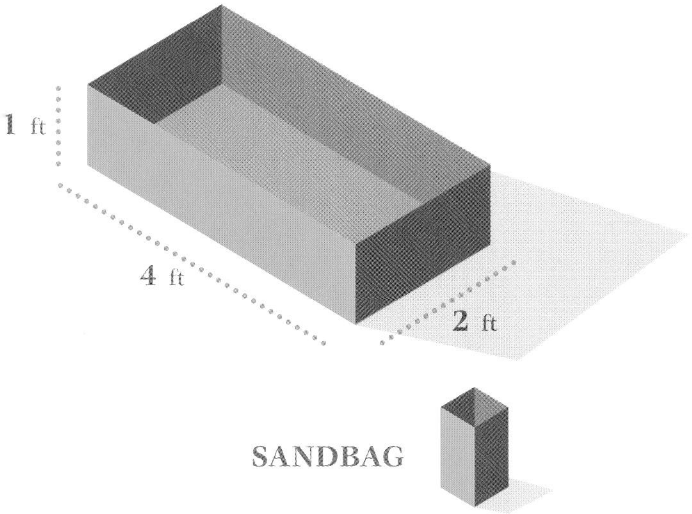

ANSWERS & INTERPRETATIONS

Score 1 point for each correct answer
Maximum score = 10

1. 11
2. 5
3. 25
4. 1 + (2 x 3); (4 + 5) - 6; (7 + 8) - 9
5. 2 bottles (or multiples of 2); 3 glasses each.
6. Double each number and add 2.
7. 72 seconds
8. ((2 x 4) ÷ 1) - 3 = 5
9. Bill
10. 32

Under 4 minutes and no incorrect answers—you have excellent numerical reasoning. You probably find that you can easily spot the best deals before buying and detect other people's numerical oversights.

Over 4 minutes or any incorrect answers—you have average numerical reasoning, and probably do most of your number-checking with a calculator. Developing this skill will give you more confidence in checking bills and invoices, and noticing any errors.

Boosting tips

1. Look for patterns in numbers. In Europe, for example, daily temperatures are measured in Celsius, not Fahrenheit. To get a temperature in Fahrenheit, multiply by 9, divide by 5, then add 32.
2. Write your own number sequence. Start with a small number (like 3), then add to it or multiply it by another number to arrive at the second number in the sequence (3 plus 4, which equals 7). Continue, using the same calculation device until you have a five-number sequence (like 3, 7, 11, 15, 16).
3. Practice putting these historical figures in chronological order: Abraham Lincoln, Julius Caesar, Cleopatra, Mao Tse-Tung.

Can you use numbers in everyday life?

There are many situations in which numerical reasoning plays an important part in our day-to-day lives. When we read labels on our food, an understanding of nutritional data can help us improve our health by allowing us to keep fat, carbohydrate, and sodium intake levels in check. If we are planning a trip to a foreign city or country, we can compare the information contained on weather charts for our destination with temperatures back home and thus pack appropriately. Likewise if we are just going away for a day and want to sightsee, we may want to find out the temperature, humidity, and chance of rain for the day. And who doesn't want to get to and from work as quickly as possible? Bus and train timetables, for example, enable us to compare transportation options with ease and confidence thus providing us with the necessary information to make favorable decisions.

TEST YOURSELF

You will need a pen and paper and a stopwatch or a clock with a second hand. Time yourself on the speed and accuracy of your answers.

1 *The table below shows the weather forecast in July for New York City and San Francisco:*

a) *What is the predicted temperature difference between New York City at midday and San Francisco at night-time?*
b) *Which city has the longest daylight hours?*
c) *If the actual humidity in San Francisco was 20% less than forecast, what would it be?*

	New York City	*San Francisco*
Temperature high	*91°F (33°C)*	*72°F (52°C)*
Temperature low	*72°F (52°C)*	*22°F (11°C)*
Relative humidity	*73%*	*85%*
Wind	*NE at 5 m.p.h. (8 k.p.h.)*	*SW at 5 m.p.h. (8 k.p.h.)*
Sunrise	*5:41 A.M.*	*6:02 A.M.*
Sunset	*8:23 P.M.*	*8:29 P.M.*
Summary	*Partly cloudy*	*Partly cloudy*

2 *The table on the right contains the relevant nutritional information for raisins:*

a) *If there are 600 raisins per 100 g, how many calories are there in each raisin?*
b) *What is the proportion of the non-carbohydrate component of raisins per 100 g?*
c) *If the recommended daily intake of fiber is 18 g, and you ate 100 g of raisins as a snack, what fraction of your recommended daily fiber intake would that represent?*
d) *What percentage of fats in raisins are saturates?*

	Per 100 g
Energy	1281 kJ (300 calories)
Protein	3.0 g
Carbohydrate	71.0 g
Sugars	71.0 g
Fat	0.7 g
Saturates	0.0 g
Fiber	6.0 g
Sodium	0.02 g

3 *Below is the early morning section of a bus timetable:*

a) *If it takes you 11 minutes to walk to work from Main Street to Central Avenue, how much quicker is the bus on a Sunday morning?*
b) *How much longer will it take you to travel from Main Street to Mountain Road on a weekday morning compared to the weekend?*
c) *Between which two stops is your journey the longest?*

	Mon–Fri	Sat & Sun
Main Street	8:12 A.M.	8:12 A.M.
Central Avenue	8:19 A.M.	8:16 A.M.
Washington Square	8:31 A.M.	8:25 A.M.
Mountain Road	8:40 A.M.	8:31 A.M.

Boosting tip

Draw up a two-column table to compare yourself as a child and an adult. Ensure that the number of rows corresponds with the amount of categories chosen: bedtime, height, distance to school/work, etc.

ANSWERS & INTERPRETATIONS

Score 1 point for each correct answer
Maximum score = 10

1. a) 69°F (22°C)
b) New York City (by 15 minutes)
c) 68%
2. a) 0.5 or 1/2 calorie
b) 29%
c) 1/3
d) 0%
3. a) 7 minutes
b) 9 minutes
c) Central Avenue and Washington Square on a weekday

Under 2 minutes and no incorrect answers—you have excellent numerical reasoning. You probably have no problem deciphering complex numerical information presented in a tabular format like performance tables and timetables.

Over 2 minutes or any incorrect answers—you have average numerical reasoning, and probably wanted to reach for a calculator! Practicing these sorts of sums in your head will help you accomplish many daily tasks more quickly and accurately.

Do you see the world through numbers?

Numerical reasoning can be improved through practice, but some people have an innate knack for numerical and logical concepts and perceive these as patterns: they instinctively perceive their world through numbers. Physicists, accountants, bankers, and actuaries require excellent numerical abilities, a comprehension of abstract analysis and functions, as well as highly developed reasoning skills, to do their jobs well.

By examining your approach to numerical situations, you will come to appreciate the role of numbers in your life. People with strong numerical intelligence usually give numbers center stage. Those who don't, see numbers only as a means to an end and avoid figures wherever they can. Numerical intelligence normally goes hand-in-hand with a love of numbers. However, if you haven't liked numbers in the past, this doesn't mean you can't come to love them.

WHAT'S YOUR ANSWER?

Choose the answers that best describe you.

1. Your bank statement arrives at the end of the month and the bottom line figure is what you were expecting:
a) You aren't surprised—you keep careful records of all expenditure and live within your means.
b) You are amazed—you've no idea how much money you spent and must just have got lucky this month.

2. You are reviewing details of new apartments, and each comes with a floor plan. You:
a) Use the dimensions given to get an accurate feel for the layout of the property.
b) Put them to one side—you would have to see the apartment before plans made any sense.

3. You are going on vacation with a group of friends, and decribe the plans to one of your colleagues. When he asks, "Who's going?" you reply:
a) With a number, giving your connection—fellow students from my dorm.
b) With names, giving each person in turn and explaining their relationship to one another.

4. Do you remember dates and unusual annniversaries more than other people?
a) Yes—I know the exact date of when I started my current job and met my best friend.
b) No—I only remember important dates like birthdays and public holidays.

Boosting tips

1. Explore numerical ways for remembering important digits in your life like your pin number. Check to see, for example, whether one number is double or half the one that either precedes or follows it. Use mathematical strategies like these as mnemonic devices.
2. Ban your calculator from your life for a week and practice doing calculations in your head.
3. Count the number of steps you take from your bedroom to your dining room, from your front door to the basement, from your desk to the photocopier at work.

5. During your journey into work, do you ever time yourself and compare progress to key landmarks along the way?
a) Yes—I keep a mental note of my "best" and "worst" times.
b) No—I'm only interested in whether I get to my desk by 9 a.m.

6. You are notified that your pay will rise by $5000 as of next month. You:
a) Work it out as a percentage increase, estimating the tax you'll have to pay to arrive at a net figure before you feel pleased or disappointed.
b) You experience elation as soon as you read "$5000."

7. When driving for pleasure, do you keep an eye on all the numerical information featured on the dashboard?
a) Yes—I always notice the speedometer, rev counter, and clock the miles I've traveled.
b) No—only the value on the speedometer.

ANSWERS & INTERPRETATIONS

Mostly a's—you don't find numbers threatening, and enjoy manipulating them for enjoyment and information. You probably get great satisfaction from creating order and balance in your personal finances.

Mostly b's—you tend to use numbers as a means to an end, rather than for pleasure. Most people fall into this category! You will probably be less anxious about math if you continue to practice the four basic operations: addition, subtraction, multiplication, and division.

Your numerical intelligence

Now that you've completed all the tests, you can profile your results to get an overall view of your strengths. Check the relevant boxes for each of your test scores.

Did you discover numbers to be a means to an end or a source of satisfaction?

- If you have 4 or more checks in the average column, you have adequate numerical intelligence. You are likely to use numbers as a tool, rather than a source of enjoyment.
- If you have 2-3 checks in either column, you have good numerical intelligence. You are likely to be confident with numbers if the situation calls for it but they wouldn't be your first choice of pastime.
- If you have 4 or more checks in the excellent column, you have superior numerical intelligence. You are likely to enjoy playing with numbers, both professionally and personally.

	Average ✓	*Excellent* ✓
Mental arithmetic		
Test 1 (pages 40-41)		
Test 2 (pages 42-43)		
Test 3 (pages 44-45)		
Numerical reasoning		
Test 1 (pages 46-47)		
Test 2 (pages 48-49)		

Developing and improving numerical intelligence

Gaining mathematical confidence is a priceless life skill. Numerically powerful people think and communicate by drawing on mathematical ideas, tools, and techniques. They can solve problems and use data systematically to develop patterns and explanations. Mathematically gifted individuals do something meaningful and purposeful with numbers and are able to apply this ability to daily living and workplace settings.

Mathematics can be one of the more intimidating school subjects because of its distinct symbolism and vocabulary. It can be challenging for teachers to bring math to life and pupils who are not confident with numbers often tend to view it as purely an intellectual pursuit with little real world relevance. This may inhibit them from accessing number sense within themselves outside of the classroom. However, such mental barriers can be overcome to reap the rich rewards that numerical intelligence bestows.

If you possess adequate-to-good numerical intelligence, remember that math is learned as a series of building-blocks with the foundation stones being addition, subtraction, multiplication, and division. Master each stage and, when you feel more confident, move on to more applied manipulations like percentages, ratios, and fractions.

If you have superior numerical intelligence, ensure that you benefit from it in all areas of life. Work out whether you're better off buying a car on the installment plan or paying for it outright, determining and paying interest, investing in stocks or property, changing your utility bills company. Apply these skills to your personal finances.

Look out for any data and numerical tables in your daily life, and think about the information you would like to extract. Shop around for loans and major purchases to get the best deals, perhaps even enter math competitions!

Working with children

Encourage children to be confident with numbers. Help them to develop numerical intelligence by nurturing their familiarity with numerical concepts. You could, for instance:

- Recite the house numbers on your street out loud to them on the way to school. Encourage youngsters to count the homes in your neighborhood, notice odd and even numbering, and speculate on missing numerals on shops or buildings.
- Bake cupcakes or cookies together. Measure out the necessary ingredients, divide up the mixture, and set the timer while the goodies are in the oven. Decorating edibles with icing and candy presents another informal and non-intimidating opportunity for counting and measuring.
- Divide up dinner portions or count money and everyday objects that you come across in a fun way.
- Play number games with cards or board games.

3

LINGUISTIC

INTELLIGENCE

What is linguistic intelligence?

SPEECH SCIENTISTS recognize four basic rules within language—phonology, syntax, semantics, and pragmatics—which linguistically intelligent people understand, apply, and manipulate skillfully.

Phonology, the sounds of words, dictates that they can rhyme with each other ("cat" and "hat") and have different spellings yet share the same pronunciation ("through" and "threw"). Syntax governs the systematic order, structure, and arrangement of words in sentences and is taught as grammar in schools. Semantics, a more applied skill, is concerned with the meaning of words and their connotations. Frequently words have to be chosen with care because small differences in construction can relay altered meanings to the ones originally intended: think of the subtleties between "simple" and "simplistic." This competence is closely linked to logical intelligence. Pragmatics is the ability to interpret intended meaning and underpins the fact that the actual words uttered are only part of the linguistic package. You also need to consider facial expression, body language, tone, inflection, and sophisticated language devices like idioms ("foot the bill" or "change of heart") when interpreting what someone is actually saying. Pragmatics is mastered late in a child's development and is linked to emotional intelligence.

Linguistic intelligence breaks down into three sub-components: communication, self-expression, and word-power skills.

Communication

Humans are essentially social beings and we have developed forms of communication that are sophisticated and unique to our species but applicable across all cultures. We communicate verbally in person, on the phone, and during video-conferencing; and non-verbally in e-mails, faxes, and letters. Our approach may be formal—when presenting at a conference or during a meeting—or informal—when chatting with friends or handwriting notes. You are constantly choosing how to best communicate with others, and your judgment impacts on your outcome.

Self-expression

Making ourselves understood is essential to communication. We all have a basic need to persuade, vent emotions, and convey feelings. The most advanced and skilled type of self-expression uses both verbal and non-verbal methods: if you want to congratulate a friend on her promotion, you would probably smile (non-verbal), say "Well done" (verbal), and give her a hug (non-verbal).

Word-power

As the basic units of language, words are governed by rules of phonology, syntax, semantics, and pragmatics. Word-power is the ability to manipulate letters and words—the linguistic equivalent of mental arithmetic. If you practice and develop word-power confidence, you can make that skill the bedrock of your linguistic intelligence.

Why is linguistic intelligence important?

Language is obviously critical to those who forge a career from it like writers and actors. But how do the rest of us actually use language? Language performs four key functions in human society. It is used:

- Rhetorically, to convince other people about our points of view or preferred course of action. This function is important for many day-to-day interpersonal interactions, as well as leadership and management situations;
- Mnemonically, as a tool for remembering information either simply by verbally labeling an object in a memorable way, or by creating a complex language device, such as an acronym, to remember a shopping list, for example;
- Didactically, for learning and teaching language as a medium, be it verbal (in class or during discussions), or non-verbal (in textbooks or academic papers);
- Metalinguistically, to use language to explain and reflect upon itself through expressions like "What do you mean?" or "Can you say that again?" We use language to talk about language.

People who are linguistically intelligent might enjoy storytelling, debating, conversing, presenting, reading aloud, dramatizing, researching topics through books, listening, or writing journal entries. Examples of professions where an understanding of words is necessary include politicians, writers, actors, editors, journalists, librarians, speech pathologists, lawyers, and radio or TV broadcasters.

How well do you use words?

Words encompass the essence of language and are the building blocks that we use to communicate. By increasing your vocabulary, and gaining familiarity with how words are constructed and manipulated, you will develop word-power and be better able to express yourself while gaining a greater understanding of different kinds of text.

There are various ways of classifying words: synonyms like "fast" and "quick" have similar meanings; antonyms like "large" and "small" have opposite meanings; palindromes like "madam" are words or phrases that read the same backward or forward. Other words, like "minute," have double meanings (a unit of time or a tiny amount).

Playing with words can be great fun, and forms the basis for many jokes and styles of humor. Journalists (whether print or TV) and editors are just two examples of jobs that require wit and a strong command of language.

TEST YOUR WORD ABILITY

1. *Russia is to rouble as France is to:*
a) franc *b)* euro *c)* peseta

2. *Which is the odd word out?*
a) cutlass *b)* cannon *c)* sword

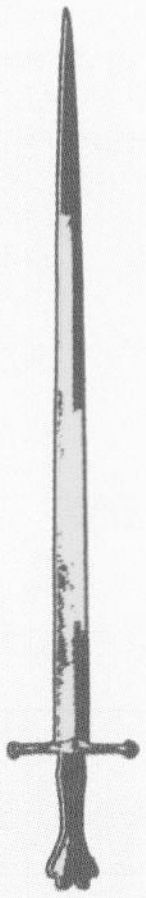

3. *Which word belongs with..?*
benevolent kind considerate
a) true *b)* malevolent *c)* generous

4. *Rearrange these letters to spell another word:*
CLEINTGLEINE

5. *Which word links these two words?*
brief (_ _ _ _) load

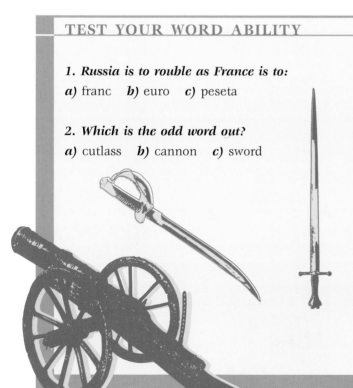

6. *Choose two words whose meanings are opposites:*
assiduous fussy lazy succinct deciduous

Boosting tips

1. Play a verbal word game with a friend or colleague whereby the first player calls out the first and last name of a famous person—Abraham Lincoln, for example. The second player names a personality whose first name starts with the same letter as the last celebrity's second name, so in this case "l" like Leonardo DiCaprio. The first player then needs to name someone whose first name starts with "c" (like Christina Rossetti). The second player now must find a name beginning with "r," but if he or she chooses someone whose first and last name begin with the same letter (i.e. Ronald Reagan), the direction of play reverses.

2. Write down any expressions and idioms that you've recently heard. Focus on each one at "word-level" and notice the creative ways in which language can be used.

7. *What do these words have in common?*

vessel cup flask vase jug

8. *What word comes next?*

ball belt bishop bomb

a) bush ***b)*** butter ***c)*** bubble

9. *Which word shares both these meanings?*

place of worship side of the head

10. *What's special about..?*

nurses run

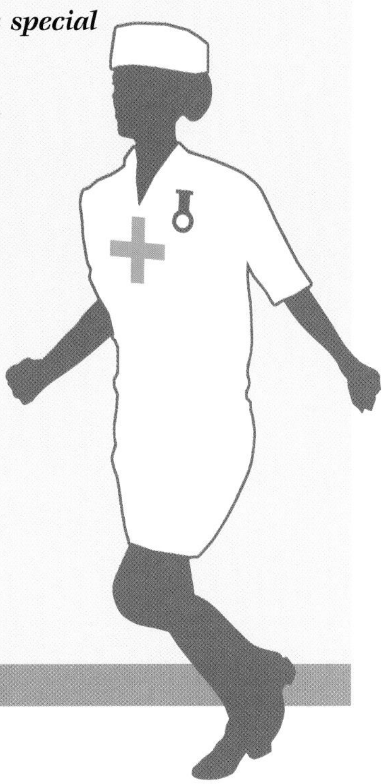

ANSWERS & INTERPRETATIONS

Score 1 point for each correct answer
Maximum score = 10

1. b)
2. b)
3. c)
4. intelligence
5. case
6. assiduous, lazy
7. They are all fluid containers.
8. c)
9. temple
10. It is a palindrome.

8 points or less—you have average word-power, and tend to view words as a functional tool rather than a creative outlet. You could develop this skill by searching for more creative ways of using words.

9 points or more—you have excellent word-power, and probably look for creative opportunities to continously play with words. You have wide vocabulary, and can see words as puzzles and games to be enjoyed and solved.

Do you have advanced word-power?

ADVANCED WORD-POWER draws on a deeper knowledge, understanding, and control of words. People gifted with this skill see words almost as letter-pattern puzzles that can be twisted and turned in amusing and clever ways. A classic example is the anagram: the letters of a word scrambled to form another word. This talent is mainly used in its purest form during leisure time, but the ability to manipulate words and deconstruct them is used by those teaching foreign languages, or those translating the spoken or written word for another audience.

Once you have discovered words to be the root of language, you are then able to delve deeper into your word-power ability. Developing this further will help you to decipher the meanings of unfamiliar words or the origins of common phrases.

TEST YOUR ABILITY

1. Which words would follow and precede these words to form new words or phrases?

stone (_ _ _ _) flower (_ _ _) time (_ _ _ _ _) option

2. How many words can you make from DREAM?

3. First remove one letter from each of the words below to make a new four-letter word. Then rearrange all of the removed letters to spell a new nine-letter word. What is it?

broad still chair paint grown
unite black boost aunts

4. Put the following four items of clothing you can wear (bras, cape, vest, tops) in the grid below in order so that the diagonal letters spell out another article of clothing.

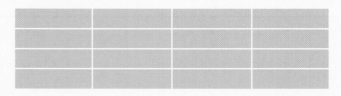

5. Create nine words from the clues in brackets. Compose a final word from the added letters.

_ _ _flet (paper) _ _imble (sewing) _ _aser (deletes)
_ _ _ kage (flood) _ _ought (idea) _ _otic (sexual)
_ _ _ der (chief) _ _rone (chair) _ _upt (volcano)

Boosting tip

Write down the first half of an opening sentence in a magazine or newspaper. Finish the sentence in as many different ways as possible. For example, if the article starts with "work-related stress can...," it could be finished with "...contribute to days lost through illness," or "...be helped by seeing a counselor," and so on. Making yourself re-use the first half of a sentence will draw on your word creativity and vocabulary.

6. *Put these animals in the correct order by filling in the blanks. What is the last word?*

snail horse sheep tiger eagle

h _ _ _ _

_

_

_ _ _ _ _

_ _

_

_

_ _ _ _ _

7. *Try these anagrams. Rearrange the letters to form a second word.*

flog tied pear pots toed

golf diet reap stop dote

ANSWERS & INTERPRETATIONS

Score 1 point for each correct answer
Maximum score = 7

1. wall—bed—share.

2. At least 10—ream, mead, red, ram, dam, dare, dame, mare, made, mad.

3. subscribe: (s)till; a(u)nts; (b)road; boo(s)t; (c)hair; g(r)own; pa(i)nt; (b)lack; unit(e).

4.

C	A	P	E
T	O	P	S
B	R	A	S
V	E	S	T

5. lea/th/er

6. sheep

7. Possible answer combinations: golf, diet, reap, stop, dote.

5 points or less—you have average advanced word-power, and may not have considered the construction or derivation of words. Developing this skill will help improve your vocabulary and fluency.

6 points or more—you have excellent advanced word-power, and use your knowledge of how words are constructed to improve your vocabulary and self-expression. You probably enjoy language and are a good all-round communicator.

Can you solve word puzzles?

USING WORDS in different ways increases your familiarity with and confidence in using them. There are numerous puzzle magazines and websites, ranging from the simple to the extremely complex, containing activities that can be used to develop word-power skills. Some puzzlers prefer particular puzzle authors, a style of game, or a level of difficulty.

Crossword puzzles are said to be the most popular and widespread word games in the world. The first known crossword to be published was created by Arthur Wynne and it appeared in an American Sunday newspaper, *The New York World*, on 21 December, 1913. Almost all newspapers on both sides of the Atlantic picked up on the idea, and the crossword puzzle as a serious adult pastime was born. Solving crosswords draws on the ability to "see" words in geometrical patterns that can be twisted and turned, and is the ultimate test of word-power.

TEST YOUR ABILITY

1. *Transport Word Search*

Find and circle 10 words that are types of transportation in the grid below. They may occur forward, backward, or diagonally. Some of the letters may be used more than once.

T	X	M	N	I	A	R	T
B	O	A	T	F	E	I	R
R	A	Y	O	E	K	J	U
E	L	T	A	X	I	E	C
M	N	R	Y	W	B	O	K
C	I	A	G	V	B	W	A
A	T	M	L	O	S	U	D
R	E	T	E	P	I	H	S

2. *Food Word Puzzle*

Fill in the blanks and work out 10 different types of food from the clues.

_ _ _ _ _ _ *(a)* _ _ _ _ _ _ _ _ _ *(b)*

_ _ _ _ _ *(c)* _ _ _ _ _ _ *(d)*

_ _ _ *(e)* _ _ _ _ _ _ _ *(f)*

_ _ _ _ _ *(g)* _ _ _ _ _ _ _ _ *(h)*

_ _ _ _ _ *(i)* _ _ _ _ _ *(j)*

Clues: Mexican corn chips (a); meat patty (b); sweet treat (c); orange vegetable (d); cured pork (e); exploded kernel (f); Italian dish (g); hot breakfast (h); bread ring (i); green leaves (j).

Boosting tips

1. Increase your vocabulary by learning a new word every day and using it in conversation. Select it from a thesaurus as an alternative to a word you overuse.

2. Play word games like Scrabble, Taboo, or Boggle.

3. Play ABC categories and generate alphabetical lists on a given topic either individually, or as a family. For example, think of a vegetable that begins with the letter "a" (asparagus), "b" (beet), "c" (carrot), and so on. Categories could include plants, children's names, TV characters, or things you would find in a garage.

3. *Animal Hangman*

Fill in the blanks from the letters shown.

a) h _ _ p _ _ _ t _ m _ s

b) o _ _ _ g _ t _ n

c) c _ _ _ c h _ _ _ a

d) _ _ l _ g _ t _ r

e) r _ _ n _ c _ _ _ s

f) _ l _ p _ _ n.t

g) s _ _ r f _ _ h

h) a _ t _ l _ p e

i) p _ r _ _ p _ _ e

j) _ r _ u _ d _ _ g

ANSWERS & INTERPRETATIONS

Score 1 point for each correct answer
Maximum score = 30

1.

T	X	M	N	I	A	R	T
B	O	A	T	F	E	I	R
R	A	Y	O	E	K	J	U
E	L	T	A	X	I	E	C
M	N	R	Y	W	B	O	K
C	I	A	G	V	B	W	A
A	T	M	L	O	S	U	D
R	E	T	E	P	I	H	S

2. a) nachos, b) hamburger, c) candy, d) carrot, e) ham, f) popcorn, g) pizza, h) pancakes, i) bagel, j) salad

3. a) hippopotamus, b) orangutan, c) chinchilla, d) alligator, e) rhinoceros, f) elephant, g) starfish h) antelope, i) porcupine, j) groundhog

***25 or less points—** you have average word-playing skills, and may not have been exposed to these sorts of word puzzles before. Being able to manipulate words skillfully is important for verbal and written self-expression. Learn to notice words and how they can be altered.*

***26 or more points—** you have excellent word-playing skills, and probably really enjoyed doing these tests. You may choose to spend your leisure time playing word games and solving word puzzles. You have a good vocabulary and think creatively to see words in various ways.*

Can you play games with words?

VERBAL COMMUNICATION is the main method of human interaction, and we spend our entire childhood learning and refining this skill. Babies babble, toddlers speak single words, pre-schoolers can put together string of words into sentences, school children chatter easily with their peers. Young children use and understand simple straightforward communication, which relies only on phonology and syntax. Adult communication is much more complex, employing semantics and pragmatics.

In order to interact successfully in the different spheres of our lives, it is necessary to refine and adapt verbal communication. When you speak to a child, address a seminar, chat with your partner, or chair a meeting, you subconsciously adjust your verbal approach to fit your audience. Your choice of vocabulary, the formality of your speech, and your use of humor will vary considerably. Practicing your communication skills in the style of situational games can help you enhance this ability.

TEST YOURSELF

Get together with a group of at least 3 friends and take turns putting yourselves in the following artificial situations. Make each seem as natural as possible.

1. Recite a nursery rhyme (i.e. the story of Humpty Dumpty) in the style of one of your closest friends.

2. Choose a famous historical figure like William Shakespeare or Pocahontas. Consider how he or she would behave, speak, and interact if that person was suddenly dropped into the 21st century. Remain in character during an entire dinner course.

3. Pick a newspaper article, a poem, or a story and read it out using the staccato delivery and rhyming sentences characteristic of rap tunes.

4. Interview yourself in the style of a chat show host. Think about differentiating your own and the interviewer's speech style, and consider the sorts of questions you would ask yourself.

5. Act out a cocktail party, where each guest has a mystery occupation, and everyone tries to guess each other's secret. Try to keep your occupation a mystery for as long as possible while truthfully answering any questions. For example, if you are a doctor, and are asked whether you wear a uniform, you might say, "Sometimes I wear a coat." You have answered honestly but have avoided commenting that the coat is white and not worn outdoors.

"The voice of the Great Spirit is heard in the mighty waters..."
"A man who has no vices has damned few virtues..."
"The lady doth protest too much, methinks..."

ANSWERS & INTERPRETATIONS

If you attempted each test and were mostly successful at carrying out instructions, you have average verbal communication. You may have found being on the spot quite stressful, and building up your confidence to speak in public will help boost this skill.

If you enjoyed doing each test, followed instructions carefully, and also managed to introduce humor and additional content, you have excellent verbal communication. You probably enjoy performing, and should consider acting as a hobby.

Boosting tip

Watch your favorite TV program or movie. Notice how scriptwriters and actors convey complex information (like emotions) about the characters.

Can you read faces?

There is more to communication than just speech: one of the more sophisticated tools comprising our repertoire is non-verbal communication. If you ask someone how they are and the reply is, "Fine, thanks," you do not subconsciously process these words at face-value. You would take in the person's tone of voice (lilting or monotonous), facial expression (happy or sad), and body language (open or closed). Non-verbal information is very revealing about the true meaning of the given response. Adding non-verbal clues to the verbal information available helps you get a fuller picture. Understanding and using non-verbal communication is a vital part of face-to-face interaction. Some jobs require this specific ability: a detective interviewing criminal suspects would be on the lookout for body language that could betray them.

As well as helping you to understand others, your non-verbal signals have an effect on those around you (such as your colleagues). Use clear, unambiguous communication signals to be understood.

TEST YOURSELF

Look carefully at the facial expressions below and match them to the emotions shown on the right:

Ashamed, surprised, anxious, disgusted, jealous.

1 ____________

2 ____________

3 ____________

Boosting tips

1. Watch a video or TV program with the volume turned down. Try to work out what is going on from the facial expressions of the protagonists.

2. Play Charades with friends, where you mime the name of a book, play, movie, or TV program. You can attempt the entire concept, for example, the play and movie *Cabaret*, where you might sit back on a chair wearing a bowler hat and mime singing, or you can break down the title into individual words or syllables.

3. Look for a mismatch between the tone of voice and what is being said. If someone says, "That's really interesting," but with a flat intonation, he or she may actually be bored. Try saying "That's terrible," but smiling, with a lilt in your voice. Practice will make you more aware of your own and others' subconscious reactions.

4

5

ANSWERS & INTERPRETATIONS

Score 1 point for each correct answer
Maximum score = 5

1. Anxious
2. Disgusted
3. Jealous
4. Ashamed
5. Surprised

3 points or less—you have average non-verbal communication, and probably pick up mixed messages from other people's spoken and body language. Remember to observe and listen to the person as a whole.

4 points or more—you have excellent non-verbal communication, and probably understand the true feelings and intentions behind people's façade. You are able to use both your body language and facial expressions to communicate skillfully.

Is the medium your message?

In addition to words and gestures, there is another layer to human language: the mode or channel. New technology means that face-to-face interaction, letters, and phone calls are no longer the only methods at our disposal; faxes, answering machines, e-mails, video conferencing, and text messaging are options, too. Each has benefits and disadvantages, and our choice of medium hinges on factors like availability, speed, immediacy, the advantages of another person being able to see you—or not—and you to see them. Never before has such wide choice been on offer! When we communicate, a sense of purpose underpins our desired outcome: we might not want to speak to someone directly because we want to avoid an argument or there isn't enough time, so we might opt for a communication method where we don't need to speak "live" and we'll leave a voicemail or send an e-mail. Considering what communication method works best, particularly for critical interactions, increases chances of success. Advertising campaigns are similar: when a new product is launched, TV commercials, press ads, and column inches represent different communication methods geared to appeal to a particular target audience.

WHAT'S YOUR ANSWER?

For each question, choose the answer which makes the best use of a given communication method.

1. Would you write a letter to:

a) Your parents to invite them for Thanksgiving.

b) A travel company to claim compensation for your vacation disaster.

2. Would you make a phone call to:

a) Discuss poor time-keeping with a member of your team.

b) Set up a meeting with a business contact.

Boosting tips

1. Keep a record of the communication methods you used over a week and consider whether you chose well. Do you rely on one particular method? Does it usually work for you or are there circumstances where an alternative approach might have yielded a better response?

2. Spend a day without sending a single e-mail. Some companies introduce "e-mail free" days to encourage staff to talk to one another face-to-face. You could propose this for your office and then offer to evaluate its business effectiveness.

ANSWERS & INTERPRETATIONS

Mostly a's—you have average communication skills, and probably found it challenging to differentiate between the more subtle communication methods. You can develop this ability by thinking about what you want to achieve from the exchange and putting yourself in the other person's shoes.

Mostly b's—you have excellent communication skills, and have a talent for skillfully choosing the most appropriate method to achieve your desired outcome. You probably obtain your goals the majority of the time, because you are a good judge of personality and can readily perceive and understand the other person's perspective.

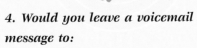

3. ***Would you see someone face-to-face to:***

a) Make a dinner reservation.

b) Negotiate terms with a client for a new contact.

4. ***Would you leave a voicemail message to:***

a) Apply for an advertised job.

b) Remind your partner that friends are coming round for dinner after work.

5. ***Would you send an e-mail to:***

a) A close friend who was devastated about a relationship split.

b) A colleague to follow up meeting action points.

Do you have a way with words?

All animal species have distinct noises and sounds, which are used to communicate location, danger, and food availability. We humans have a wide variety of ways to express ourselves. Although newborn babies can only cry to signal a need for food, warmth, or comfort, astute parents can ascertain the difference and respond accordingly.

Humans have evolved highly sophisticated speech which is planned and organized to achieve specific end results. We deliberately choose our words and how we put them together adding devices like humor to achieve depth and add color to language. This type of eloquence will help you to better communicate ideas or feelings to others, who will then be more able to understand what it is you want or need. This is a skill we can continue to develop throughout life.

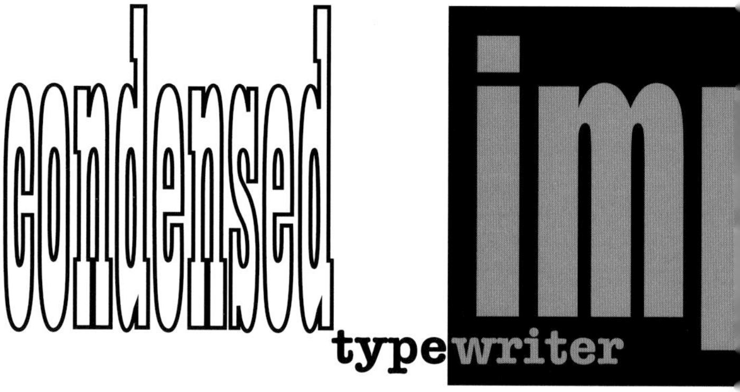

WHAT'S YOUR ANSWER?

Which of the two options would you choose?

1. You're at a dinner party to celebrate your friend's birthday, and the host suddenly asks you to say a few words. Would you:

a) Panic and propose a quick toast.

b) Amuse everyone with the story of how you met and raise your glass after a moving invitation to drink to his or her happiness.

2. Arriving at the kindergarten to pick up your niece, her teacher asks you to entertain the other children by telling them a story while she gets her. Would you:

a) Pick a well-known story like *Goldilocks*.

b) Invent an imaginative tale of dragons and princesses to keep the children in suspense.

Boosting tips

1. Increase the range of your vocabulary by picking up a different word at random from the dictionary before you go into work every day. Learn its meaning and its pronunciation. Use it during the day in conversations with colleagues.

2. Increase your verbal fluency. Think of dictionary definitions for words you see on your way to work—on signs, in newspapers, and in shop windows. How would you define words like "freeway," "war," or "trousers?"

3. You are asked to learn a poem by heart. Would you:

a) Keep writing it down until you memorize it.

b) Continue to recite it aloud until you are letter-perfect.

4. You come home from work. When you flick on the light switch, friends and family yell "Surprise!" as they have organized a secret birthday party for you. Would you:

a) Immmediately try to shift attention away from yourself.

b) Never lose your composure and make a confident speech to thank everyone who organized the party.

5. Your boss asks you to present your project findings to the management team. Would you:

a) Feel anxious about standing up in front of all those people.

b) Look forward to it as public speaking is your forte.

6. Are you known as a great story- or joke-teller among your friends and colleagues?

a) No, I tend to do the listening.

b) Yes, I enjoy being a raconteur.

ANSWERS & INTERPRETATIONS

Mostly a's—you have average verbal self-expression, and may find it difficult to articulate your thoughts at short notice, or to convey more complicated ideas to others. Improve by rehearsing for meetings or social events, so that you have some verbal set pieces to fall back on.

Mostly b's—you have excellent verbal self-expression, and can articulate complex thoughts spontaneously. You are probably known for your quick-wittedness and verbal sparring. You are able to produce a coherent and eloquent response to most situations.

Can you write about yourself?

LIKE ITS VERBAL equivalent, written self-expression is used in all areas of life. In our personal lives, we leave notes for family members, instructions for the babysitter, write letters and postcards, and keep diaries. Professionally, we write memos, e-mails, reports, and letters to colleagues and clients. Success at home and at work often depends on our ability to accurately and appropriately communicate our ideas in writing. Journalists and novelists make a living from creative writing and are skilled at adapting their style of prose for an intended audience.

In contrast with its verbal equivalent, written self-expression can be for a public or a private audience. Sometimes we write just for ourselves in the form of a diary or private poem. At other times, we write a personal letter to just one recipient. Professional authors write for public consumption and thrive on their work being read by a mass audience.

TEST YOURSELF

Prepare the following tasks at home on your own. Get three other friends to do the same. Arrange for everyone to type up their assignments before you get together. Place all descriptions face up on the table and attempt to match each ad to its writer.

Task 1

Write a personal ad, starting with a description of yourself, followed by information on the type of person you would like to meet. Think about whether you would describe yourself physically or emotionally, whether you are looking for fun or commitment, and the ideal qualities you seek in a prospective partner.

Task 2

Write a commercial describing your personality as a new car model. Think about how you would summarize who you are in terms of style (A), market sector (B), performance (C), color (D), and target audience (E).

Boosting tips

1. Reading is a great way of improving your written self-expression because you can appraise how others express themselves. If you want to improve your business writing, re-read a report that made an impact. If you want to improve your creative writing, read through a poem or a short story that you particularly enjoyed. Make a list of why you think these pieces of writing work so well.

2. Buy a pack of blank greeting cards so that you can express your own sentiments rather than signing your name below someone else's words. Varying the writing style or choosing unusual card-giving occasions will stretch your written self-expression skills in interesting ways.

ANSWERS & INTERPRETATIONS

If only some of your friends guessed your identity from what you wrote, you have average written self-expression, and may rely on verbal self-expression to communicate with others. Developing your written communication will enhance your career and widen the tools you have to express yourself. Try sending an e-mail when you would normally make a phone call.

If all your friends guessed your identity from what you wrote, you have excellent writing skills, and probably enjoy expressing yourself in the written form, both at work and in your private life. You should develop this gift by writing creatively as a hobby.

Can you deliver a good speech?

One of the most challenging linguistic tests is public speaking because communication is usually one way: you are talking and the audience is listening, and you are unlikely to receive any verbal feedback until your speech actually ends. This makes for an unnatural, often challenging, interaction.

Before writing a speech, it is important to identify the goal of your presentation. Do you want to share information or persuade? Think about who will be sitting in your audience before you research your chosen topic. When you sit down to write the speech, devote attention to the introduction and the conclusion as these will set the tone and provide general structure. When you come to perform your speech, decide how formal or casual you want your style to be and choose presentation aids accordingly.

Confident public speaking is a key skill in business and academia, particularly at senior level. Outside of work, this ability is most often called upon at family gatherings, weddings, or anniversaries. Everyone remembers a great speech as it captured their attention, and it could be your turn the next time.

TEST YOURSELF

You've been asked to speak at your friend Chris's wedding. Below are the key facts. Place them in the correct order and use this information as the basis for your speech script. Perform the speech out loud, alone or to a friend, as if you were delivering it before an audience for real.

1. His first apartment was just around the corner from his office and had a leaky roof, which often flooded when it rained.
2. Chris was born on 21 April 1968 during a thunderstorm in Chicago.
3. He met Megan, his wife-to-be, at a sports writers' convention. It was love at first sight.
4. His parents moved to Seattle, where Chris went to school and swam competitively.
5. The wedding theme decision was left to you.
6. You met at college where you both played for the basketball team.
7. Chris introduced you to Megan one week after they first met.
8. Chris went to college in San Francisco, majoring in Geography.
9. Chris proposed the following Christmas.
10. His first job was writing for a sports magazine in New York.

Boosting tips

1. Write down five unusual topics on different pieces of paper. Fold each one up and put them all in your pocket. During the day, when you have some free time, take one out and talk for five minutes on the subject. Try this out on your own and with others around you.

2. Memorable, informative, and entertaining speeches rely on anecdotes, stories, and unusual facts to keep audiences interested. Keep a notebook of tales or clippings that have caught your eye, collect them, and use them to pepper future speeches.

ANSWERS & INTERPRETATIONS

The correct order of the speech is 2–4–8–6–10–1–3–7–9–5 which corresponds to the chronological order of events.

If you came up with this order or similar, and added extra anecdotes or humor, you have excellent self-expression skills, and can construct a speech to hold an audience's attention. You probably give presentations at work, or enjoy offering toasts at family gatherings.

If you didn't place your facts in the correct order, nor added any embellishments to your speech, you have average self-expression. Lots of people are anxious about speaking in public, so you are not alone. Practice saying something often—no matter how short—to get used to holding attention with your voice.

Your linguistic intelligence

NOW THAT YOU'VE completed all the tests, you can profile your results to get an overall view of your strengths. Check the relevant boxes for each of your test scores.

Did you discover words to be a source of pleasure, or just a communication conduit?

- If you have 7 or more checks in the average column, you have adequate linguistic intelligence. You are likely to use words and language as a tool, rather than as a source of amusement.
- If you have 3-4 checks in either column, you have good linguistic intelligence. You are likely to be confident with words if this is required, but wouldn't choose to play with words if given the choice.

	Average ✓	*Excellent* ✓
WORD-POWER		
***Test 1* (pages 58-59)**		
***Test 2* (pages 60-61)**		
***Test 3* (pages 62-63)**		
COMMUNICATION		
***Test 1* (pages 64-65)**		
***Test 2* (pages 66-67)**		
***Test 3* (pages 68-69)**		
SELF-EXPRESSION		
***Test 1* (pages 70-71)**		
***Test 2* (pages 72-73)**		
***Test 3* (pages 74-75)**		

- If you have 7 or more checks in the excellent column, you have superior linguistic intelligence. You are likely to enjoy language games and see words as a source of pleasure.

Developing and improving linguistic intelligence

Language is a universal tool, which allows us to communicate, persuade, learn, instruct, and entertain. Developing your linguistic abilities should be fun and rewarding, so keep focused on those specific areas that you would like to improve, and consider what you want to gain from developing them. Do you want to express yourself well in meetings? Feel more confident about speaking in public? Find an outlet for your creativity? Write authoritative reports or letters?

If you possess adequate-to-good linguistic intelligence, which are stronger—your oral or written skills? People often find that one skill comes to them more naturally than the other. If you speak more fluently than you write, try developing a prose style that reflects the way you talk. If you enjoy deliberating over your choice of words when writing, try relaxing more in your verbal communication.

If you have superior linguistic intelligence, focus on a particular language art form, like poetry, and develop it in your spare time. Enroll in a creative writing course, explore different poetic styles, attend readings, and create your own compositions. Some poetry clubs even have "open mike" sessions, where people are encouraged to perform their work and discuss it with others. You could, for instance:

- Keep a journal and practice your written language skills by daily allocating time to put pen to paper. Select a particular style of prose and set yourself a target number of written words per day. Write in epistolary form, as a novel, a play, a progress report, or a biography. Include descriptions of places you have visited, stories of people you have met, and scripts of conversations you have had.
- If you would like to improve your verbal ability, organize a debating evening with friends. Choose a controversial topic: draw up for and against arguments on a flipchart with a friend with each of you representing the opposing side. Your challenge is to win the rest of the group over to your point of view. Make sure that everyone takes a vote at the beginning and at the end to see who's been swayed.

Working with children

As parents or teachers we want to teach youngsters how to express themselves and understand others. Children naturally enjoy playing with words by telling jokes, using rhyme, and making up nonsense words. You could further this innate enthusiasm by:

- Learning a foreign language together. Buy a phrasebook, and memorize a dozen basic words or phrases. Use these in place of your first language when you're at home together.
- Encouraging reading in a whole range of written formats: comics, magazines, road signs, restaurant menus, even the TV guide.

4

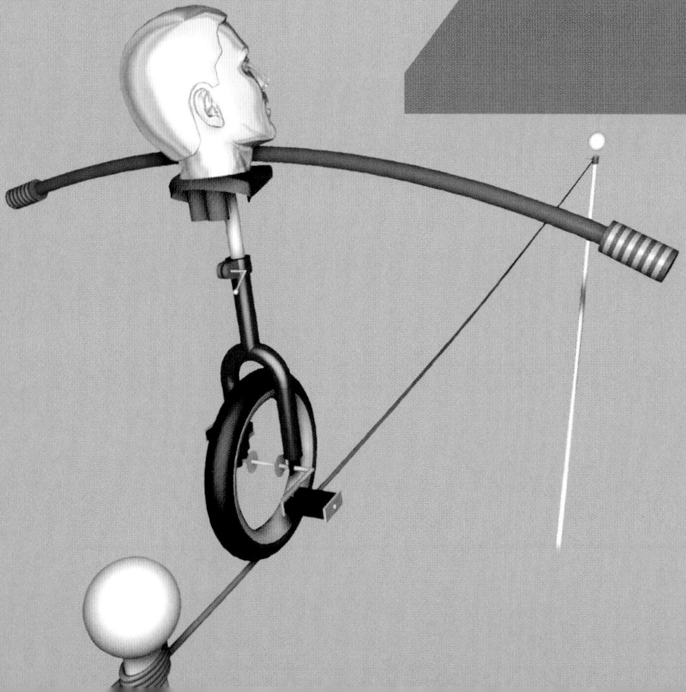

EMOTIONAL

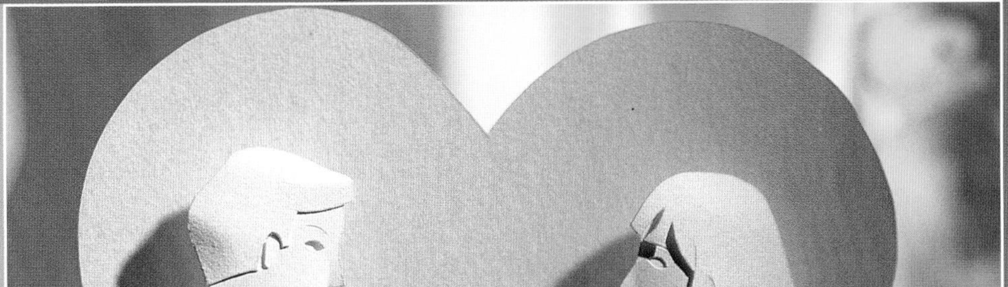

INTELLIGENCE

What is emotional intelligence?

THE TERM emotional intelligence may seem like a recently coined buzzword, but Howard Gardner identified it as one of his seven multiple intelligences back in 1983. In 1995, Daniel Goleman's book, *Emotional Intelligence: Why It Can Matter More Than IQ*, caused a stir becoming an international bestseller overnight and introducing the concept of emotional intelligence to people outside of academia, with whom the concept struck a deep chord. It has since been embraced by the educational system and the world of business and finance as a core skill for success.

The key elements of emotional intelligence are:

- Appreciating emotions in others, characterized by an aptitude for connecting and interacting with people by understanding, empathizing, and responding appropriately to their feelings. Such people make good team players, dependable partners, and popular friends.
- Negotiating solutions, having the capacity to detect, deflect, and manage potential arguments or discords to the advantage of everyone involved. People with this ability make good managers or negotiators, and enjoy great personal relationships.
- Handling relationships, the skill at managing emotions in other people by detecting and tuning into given moods or motives to read the subtler undercurrents. Such people make excellent listeners and leaders.

All of these elements invitably come into play with every emotional relationship in our life, be it with partners, parents, siblings, or work colleagues.

Partner relationships

Escalating divorce rates mean less and less people are willing to stay in unhappy marriages. In today's world, the emotional connection between couples needs to be strong if a union is not only to survive, but actually flourish. Constructive emotional communication lies at the core of a successful partnership.

Family relationships

The first relationship we have is with our parents: initially on their terms. As we get older, this bond can become increasingly difficult to sustain and manage, so compromise and honest communication on both sides is crucial for healthy and satisfying family relationships. Parents need to accept that their children will inevitably grow up. Grown-up children need to accept that parents are not infallible.

Social relationships

Now that the extended family support network is less prevalent, good social relationships are key. Many of us view our close friends as pivotal to our emotional wellbeing but, from a wider perspective, the ability to fit into different social groups is equally important. Striking up a conversation with strangers at a dinner party, befriending other parents at a child's birthday party, or mixing with colleagues at the annual company conference—these activities all require the ability to accurately read social and emotional cues.

Professional relationships

A wealth of research into emotional intelligence and job performance has arisen as companies seek the edge over competitors in terms of people, their most valuable asset. The concept of emotional intelligence has become so relevant in today's business world that assessments and development programs are now standard practice. The ability to lead and motivate staff, or negotiate with and persuade customers, are both emotional talents.

Emotionally intelligent people are skilled at teamwork, cooperation, and resolving conflict. They are more assertive, popular, skilled at communicating, considerate, and better at solving emotional problems.

Why is emotional intelligence important?

Emotional intelligence is a valuable tool for any kind of private or public social interaction. The benefits of having strong and secure personal relationships are evident, and most people would admit to wanting to be fulfilled in this area. Applying these skills in the workplace can also bring satisfaction: managers and colleagues with superb emotional intelligence are able to glean the best from their team, motivate staff, give (and receive) constructive feedback, and gain loyalty. These workers are an asset to organizations both in financial and performance terms.

Examples of people who need excellent emotional intelligence include teachers, counselors, actors, sales people, managers, and those in the social services.

Do you and your partner communicate?

In the last 10 years, much has been written about the differences in communication between men and women; for example, from an early age, girls play cooperatively while boys play competitively. It is socially acceptable for females to show emotion, whereas males are generally taught to hide theirs. Men and women enter relationships with disparate capacities for emotional awareness, different expectations of emotional fulfillment, and divergent tools for managing feelings. This causes problems like a lack of communication (from the inability or reluctance to say what one really means or feels); unresolved negative feelings (from previous incidents); and current pessimism (from negative past experiences). Effective communication and listening skills are vital to a healthy relationship.

TEST YOUR COMMUNICATION SKILLS

You and your partner should each answer the appropriate questions with a "yes" or a "no" answer, then count up each one's "yes" responses separately.

Partner questions

1. Would your partner talk about his or her feelings as freely as about his or her new car?

2. Does your partner listen when you talk?

3. Can your partner tell if you're upset?

4. Do you criticize your partner and/or his or her behavior when you argue?

5. When you talk, does your partner ask questions to get deeper into the issue?

6. Does your partner ask you what you want during intimacy, or say what he or she would like?

7. Does your partner initiate discussions about money and your joint finances?

8. Does your partner chat to friends or family on the phone?

9. Does your partner ever praise you?

10. Does your partner say or show he or she loves you at least once a week?

Your questions

1. Do you talk to your partner about the little things that get you down?

2. Do you listen when your partner talks?

Boosting tip

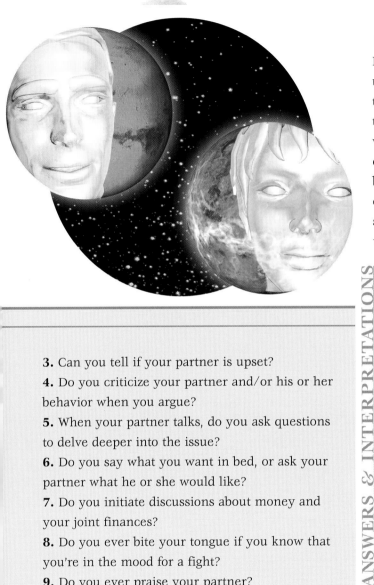

Learn to discuss the day's events with your partner using the three-minute listening rule: he or she talks for three minutes while you listen; then you talk for three minutes while he or she listens. You will hear much more of what the other person is communicating if you can't interrupt or be distracted by what *you* want to say next. Good listeners ask open-ended questions, concentrate on what is being said, don't interrupt, or make presumptions about unexpressed feelings or intent.

3. Can you tell if your partner is upset?
4. Do you criticize your partner and/or his or her behavior when you argue?
5. When your partner talks, do you ask questions to delve deeper into the issue?
6. Do you say what you want in bed, or ask your partner what he or she would like?
7. Do you initiate discussions about money and your joint finances?
8. Do you ever bite your tongue if you know that you're in the mood for a fight?
9. Do you ever praise your partner?
10. Do you say or show you love your partner at least once a week?

ANSWERS & INTERPRETATIONS

If one or both of you scored 3 or less "yes" responses—you have average communication skills and probably often have blazing arguments or leave things unsaid to avoid conflict. If you both work on this aspect of your relationship, you will improve how you deal with each other and others.

If one or both of you scored between 3-6 "yes" responses—you have good communication skills and probably talk about most things quite easily, although one or two topics may be difficult to broach. Try tackling these subjects together when you are both feeling calm.

If one or both of you scored 7 or more "yes" responses—you have excellent communication skills and your relationship is likely to be a close and secure one. Keep up the good work.

If you and your partner are in different score bands—you probably get by because one of you is compensating for the other's lack of emotional communication.

What is your conflict style?

THERE IS a big difference between healthy conflict and the sort of strife that can ultimately destroy a relationship. Such altercations are perceived as criticism and personal attacks. Over time, they can build up negative equity in a relationship. Arguments that start with "you never" or "you always" are classic examples of this. You may feel overworked, but actually shout, "You never tidy up!" to your partner. Or you might scream, "We always have to go to the restaurant you choose!" when deep down you feel undervalued. Strong partnerships are able to open up discussions beyond the initial, emotionally charged accusations. Every couple has their own conflict style: by understanding the way that you and your partner argue, you can develop a stronger and closer bond.

TEST YOUR CONFLICT STYLE

Choose the answers that best describe you (or your partner where applicable).

1. *How would you and your partner typically end an argument?*
a) One of us would change the subject so we were on friendly terms again.
b) One of us would walk out, but we'd make up later that same day.
c) We would reach a compromise.

2. *What do you and your partner see as the purpose of an argument?*
a) We try to avoid arguing.
b) To let off steam.
c) To talk about any differences before they become a major problem.

3. *If your partner said, "Let's agree to disagree," what would your reaction be?*
a) You would accept his or her peace offering without a second thought.
b) You would not see this statement as a reason to stop arguing.
c) You would rather arrive at a conclusion where you both reached agreement.

4. *When you and your partner are arguing, is he or she more likely to:*
a) Retreat into stony silence.
b) Raise his or her voice, pace the room, or gesticulate wildly.

Boosting tip

Think back to the last three fights that you've had with your partner. Make a note of the trigger, what you argued about, and the outcome. Are you still bothered about what provoked the fight? Is there a recurring pattern?

c) Continue, until he or she feels you have seen his or her point of view.

5. When you and your partner are quarreling, are you more likely to:

a) Deflect the argument as you feel uncomfortable with extreme displays of emotion.
b) Remember a series of unrelated grievances halfway through and air those, too.
c) Try to get him or her to agree with you.

ANSWERS & INTERPRETATIONS

*Mostly a's—your conflict style is avoidance.** You and your partner shirk away from having arguments (which you may see as a sign of compatibility) to avoid creating bad feeling. You ask open questions (those that can't simply be answered by a "yes" or "no" answer) as a way of getting information from your partner. This style may suit your personalities, but be wary of it as a sign of low self-esteem, or fear of breaking up.*

*Mostly b's—your conflict style is volatile.** You and your partner's arguments are passionate and intense. You see arguing as an outlet for emotional steam and probably thrive on the excitement that fights bring to the relationship, but ensure that such drama is not compensating for a lack of companionship or mutual interests. Try paraphrasing your emotional accusations as "When you...it makes me feel..." to lower the confrontational tone.*

*Mostly c's—your conflict style is resolution.** You and your partner's arguments are not fiery or emotional, and you quarrel only occasionally to talk about any differences as a way of remaining close. You probably use closed questions (those that force a "yes" or "no" response) as a way of getting to the heart of an issue. Make sure there is still a place for passion in your relationship.*

*** John Gottman, Professor of Psychology at the University of Washington, Seattle, identified three strong conflict styles among partners—avoidance, volatile, and resolution.**

What are your relationship weaknesses?

IT CAN OFTEN be difficult to identify those factors that, over time, weaken and damage a relationship. If you have had a series of relationship failures, being a poor judge of character may not have been the only component. If you are going through another bad patch in a current relationship, you may be repeating patterns of destructive behavior. Do you tend to finish relationships first? Do you tend to be the one to get dumped? Are you systematically attracted to people older or younger than yourself? Are you drawn to "dangerous" or unpredictable individuals? There are many facets and types of relationship pitfalls. Identifying your key relationship risk is the first step to a fulfilling, safe, and happy love life.

TEST YOURSELF

Put these statements in the order that they apply to you and past relationships.

1. I feel anxious that my partner is too good for me, or will leave me.
2. I tend to make "always" and "never" accusations during arguments.
3. I feel our relationship is comfortable but not exciting.
4. I find it easier to think of five things that irritate me about my partner, instead of five good points.
5. I feel unhappy with our sex life, but can't face talking about it.
6. I think of our relationship as just "going through the motions."

Boosting tips

1. Ask a close friend to pick out three adjectives that describe the sort of partners you go for. Such impartial insight from someone who knows you well could be very informative.

2. Make a list of the qualities that a perfect partner ought to have. Draw up another list of the different ways you would behave in an ideal relationship. Use these lists as your blueprint for happiness in the future.

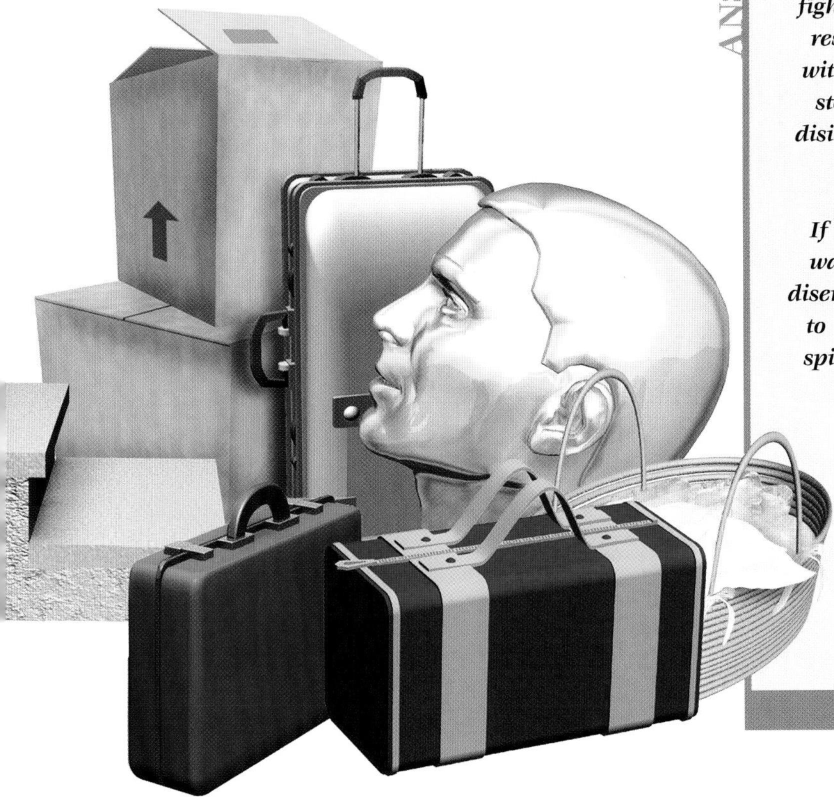

ANSWERS & INTERPRETATIONS

If 1 and/or 5 were in your top 3 statements—watch out for security craving. People who desire constant reassurance often have low self-esteem, and are always looking for external signs of their worth, which is draining for their partners. If you feel that your partner is too good for you, he or she may start to believe this is true and leave. Boost your self-esteem from within and get stimulation and support from outside your relationship.

If 2 and/or 4 were in your top 3 statements—watch out for constant criticism. People who inundate their partners with faults do not prioritize complaints, which makes their partners less likely to respond to the really important matters. If you criticize constantly, pick your fights carefully. Some people, particularly men, resist shouting matches by "stone-walling," or withdrawing from a conflict with silence and a stony expression. This sends out messages of disinterest, but is also a mechanism for shutting down to prevent further hurt.

If 3 and/or 6 were in your top 3 statements—watch out for disillusionment. People who are disenchanted with their liaisons have lost the will to make things work and the relationship may spiral into breakdown. If you are disappointed with your loved one, make a place for appreciation and affection. Try to recall what you loved about him or her when you first met.

Are your parents friends or foes?

Our relationship with our parents begins before birth, when attachment, or an emotional bond, first forms. This connection dominates early childhood, but as we mature into adults, relationships with siblings, friends, and partners gradually become our major source of security and comfort, even though our parents retain a unique role. Healthy and close family relationships are full of affection.

Adult child—parent relationships work like a two-way street. The adult child must be willing to accept that his or her parents are individuals with positive qualities, needs, but also failings. Parents, in turn, need to accept grown-up children as adults, free to make their own decisions, often with different perspectives and priorities. Accept them as human beings who happen to be your parents.

TEST YOUR RELATIONSHIP

Check the FOUR statements that most apply to you and your parents.

- ☐ **1.** My parents love me and are proud of me.
- ☐ **2.** I have little in common with my parents.
- ☐ **3.** My parents want to know more about my life than I'm willing to reveal.
- ☐ **4.** I often turn to my parents for advice or support.
- ☐ **5.** My parents criticize and undermine me.
- ☐ **6.** I feel that I have to protect my parents from certain aspects of my life.
- ☐ **7.** My parents are loyal and supportive of me.
- ☐ **8.** I wish my parents would show more interest in my life.
- ☐ **9.** My parents still see me and treat me as a child.
- ☐ **10.** I enjoy spending time with my parents.

Boosting tips

1. Make a list of the things that you would like to change about your relationship with your parents. Cross out those things that you are unable to change because they are a factor of either your or your parents' temperament or personality. Come up with a plan for changing what's left.
2. Invite your parents over for a meal. Create a peaceful ambience with gentle music and scented candles and make a special effort with the food.
3. Reminisce over old photos together. If they mainly remind you of good times, keep hold of those feelings; if they mainly conjure up bad memories, learn to let go and move on.

ANSWERS & INTERPRETATIONS

Total the number of points for the four statements most applicable to you and your parents.

1. 10 points; 2. 2 points; 3. 5 points;
4. 10 points; 5. 2 points; 6. 5 points;
7. 10 points; 8. 2 points; 9. 5 points;
10. 10 points

Under 20 points—you are not particularly close to your parents and are likely to turn to others for security and comfort. You may be carrying over grudges from childhood, or are currently experiencing conflict with your parents, so look for a new direction in your relationship: focus on the people you have become, not who you were 10 or 20 years ago. Try to find a common interest or something that you all enjoy doing.

Between 20 and 30 points—you are fairly well-attached to your parents, but this is supplemented by emotional closeness from other relationships. Families, for example, have unwritten codes of conduct. A common rule is not to express anger, although this can be detrimental within a family. The chances are you are still abiding by these principles, so identifying them can help change the ways that you experience and express your emotions.

Over 30 points—you have a very secure attachment to your parents and feel cherished and valued. This has been the blueprint for the formation of other secure and loving relationships. Try to preserve the quality of this bond throughout your lives because grandchildren, ill health, and aging can add strain to even good family relationships.

Do you get along with your siblings?

SIBLING RELATIONSHIPS are formed during childhood when our emotional focus widens beyond our parents. The initial nature of these relationships is carried through to adult life: siblings who were close, played well together, and enjoyed each other's company, usually move into adulthood providing companionship and emotional support for each other. Those who competed and fought with one another are likely to continue with this behavior pattern.

The relationship between brothers and sisters, however, is dynamic in nature and changes to financial or social status can often cause tension between or among siblings: a younger brother's sudden rise in status or overnight success may cause a glitch in the relationship with his older brother. Whether this friction is resolved amicably or not, depends on the maturity and adaptability of both parties. Siblings who remain in contact provide a mutually stable, long-lasting, and valuable support network for one another.

TEST THE STRENGTH OF YOUR SIBLING RELATIONSHIP(S)

Which of the three options best describes you and your sibling(s)? If you have more than one, you might like to answer the questions separately for each brother or sister.

1. *Your mother breaks her leg and is taken to the emergency room. You:*
a) Might bump into each other in the hospital reception area.
b) Ensure that one of you visits your mother each day.
c) Go and see your mother together the next morning followed by lunch so you can sit down to plan a visiting rotation.

2. *Do you see your sibling(s) as:*
a) Someone you knew as a child.
b) A family member.
c) A friend.

3. *Your sibling is hard up financially. Would you:*
a) Keep a distance—it's none of your business.
b) Talk to other family members about the best way to offer support.
c) Lend whatever money was needed, if possible.

Boosting tips

1. Call up your sibling(s) and arrange to see him, her, or them without partners, children, or parents. Rediscover yourselves as the adults that you now are.

2. Draw a relationship map of your immediate family, with you at the center. Use different colors (red for conflict, green for closeness, blue for indifference) to map the direction of your relationship with individual close family members, and evaluate the quality of your bond. Can you see any trends? Is your family strong or under strain? Are your relationships typical of your family unit?

4. Do you compete for your parents' attention?

a) Yes. *b)* Sometimes. *c)* Never.

5. If distance was no object, would you:

a) See each other once a year.

b) See each other once a month.

c) See each other once a week.

6. Do you stay in touch because:

a) Your parents arrange get-togethers.

b) Blood is thicker than water.

c) Because you want to.

ANSWERS & INTERPRETATIONS

Mostly a's—you have an acquaintance-based relationship with your sibling(s). You are rarely in contact and feel rather indifferent about him, her, or them. Is this the result of a falling out (in which case, endeavor to make up), or of drifting apart (in which case, make an effort to get to know one another as adults)? Sibling relationships become more important as parents are less able to provide the emotional glue that binds families.

Mostly b's—you have a family-based relationship with your sibling(s), maintain regular contact, attend and organize family gatherings, and would support each other in times of need. You may, however, be straining yourself to keep disparate parties together as your family motto underlines the importance of sticking together.

Mostly c's—you have a friendship-based relationship with your sibling(s), which is close and caring, and you got on well together as children. While you are both fortunate to have such lifelong support in each other, remember that some sibling relationships are at the exclusion of all others. Therefore ensure that you maintain good relationships with your partner and friends as well.

Can you relate to children?

RAISING CHILDREN is the most important role we have as parents. We initiate our children into being physically independent by teaching them how to read, write, and get dressed. Finding the right way to teach a child how to be emotionally alert, however, is often harder.

Children are great mimics and learn by example, so the best way of teaching them emotional intelligence is by showing it in your dealings with them and other people. Feeling frustrated, confused, or anxious are natural feelings—if parents never seem to have a bad day, children might grow up suppressing all negative emotions which is unhealthy as well as unnatural. As an adult, you can separate your feelings from your actions—this distinction is critical for future emotional wellbeing—and children with a high degree of emotional intelligence are more popular, secure, happier, and better prepared to face the world.

TEST YOUR ABILITY

Imagine this situation: you collect your child after school and he or she is visibly upset. After some coaxing, your child names a classmate who has been picking on him or her during recess. How would you react if you know that:

1. ***The two children are friends.***
2. ***The other child has a reputation for bullying.***
3. ***Your child can be physically boisterous.***

From the options opposite, pick out the THREE responses for each of the above scenarios that best summarize the way that you would deal with the situation.

Boosting tips

1. You and your child can become emotionally in tune with each other by using the "stop—think—act" traffic light analogy. Stop and calm down when the situation gets out of hand (red light); consider what you are feeling and what the best course of action should be (yellow light); then act on a plan (green light). Practice and apply this together.
2. Set time aside with your children every day to discuss how school went.

A. Try to smooth things over by buying your child candy on the way home.
B. Tell your child to stand up for himself or herself and give as good as he or she gets.
C. Talk to your child about the background to the argument and try to discover the cause.
D. Tell your child he or she must have done something to provoke the other child.
E. Talk to your child about how he or she felt.
F. Change the subject—you don't want to make a mountain out of a molehill.
G. Tell your child to find a teacher the next time it happens.
H. Talk to your child about how the other child might be feeling.

ANSWERS & INTERPRETATIONS

Your choice of response will obviously vary according to your parenting style and your child's temperament.

If you did NOT choose c), e), g), or h)—you have average emotional intelligence, and may have been focused on your own feelings rather than your child's. Emotional upset presents a useful opportunity to validate and talk about feelings with children.

If your choice included c), e), g), or h)—you have good emotional intelligence and may have modeled your own feelings in an emotionally intelligent way, or thought about the child's, but perhaps did not match up the two. Be a mediator, not an arbitrator: if you intervene to pass judgment, youngsters won't have ownership of the outcome, are less likely to abide by the final outcome, and won't develop the skills to resolve conflict on their own.

If you chose THREE out of c), e), g), and h)—you have excellent emotional intelligence, both in dealing with your child and in showing him or her how to manage his or her emotions. You are showing interest and empathy for the child by finding out more about the situation through his or her feelings, which you deem to be important. Any action that follows is more likely to be seen by the child as fair because you took the time to investigate. In recognizing the child's emotion, you have offered an appropriate solution to the problem.

Are you a good friend?

THERE ARE THREE major aspects to achieving success in social relationships. The first is an ability to manage your own emotions and to express them in the right way. The second is an aptitude for empathizing with others: putting yourself in their emotional "shoes" and establishing a mutual understanding. The third skill—handling emotions in others—is the capacity to correctly interpret other people's emotions as directed toward you, deflecting them, if necessary, and is the most difficult one to acquire. If you develop these three abilities, you will know when to speak your mind and when not to, how to change someone's mood for the better, and how to anticipate problem areas in your friendships and be clear about the best ways of working them out.

TEST YOURSELF

Choose the answers that best describe you.

1. A really close friend starts a new job and doesn't return any of your calls. Would you:
a) Feel deeply offended.
b) Wonder if he or she is OK.
c) E-mail him or her instead.

2. Your friend's partner makes a pass at you. Would you:
a) Go along with it for a giggle.
b) Flatly reject the advances.
c) Discreetly tell him or her that you're not interested.

3. You're in the middle of dinner with your friend at her apartment when she takes an extended call from another friend who is experiencing a relationship crisis. Would you:
a) Feel he or she is being rude to you and slip out the door.
b) Finish your meal and settle down with a magazine while you wait for him or her to finish.
c) Put both plates in the fridge so you can both continue your evening together once the crisis has blown over.

4. Your friend earns a lot less than you. When planning a night together, would you:
a) Offer to pay for him or her.
b) Invite him or her over for a meal at your place.
c) Negotiate your night out around his or her budget.

5. You lend your friend an item of clothing which comes back damaged. Would you:
a) Refuse his or her excuses.
b) Wait for his or her explanation before lashing out.
c) Accept his or her apology.

Boosting tips

1. Spend one day writing down your self-talk (inner dialog) as it pops into your head. Re-word each phrase in a positive way, challenge your negative thoughts, or reinforce good feelings.

2. Reflect on group dynamics at work. Rank each person in your team in terms of popularity, his or her emotional management ability, and your emotional closeness to them.

ANSWERS & INTERPRETATIONS

Mostly a's—you think about your own emotions, but find it hard to manage them. You should try "getting in touch" with your feelings, and thinking about how best to act. People who take control of their emotions take control of their lives.

Mostly b's—you are largely in touch with your own emotions and have strong, established, lasting friendships. You usually notice other people's emotions, but sometimes miss the more subtle social signals.

Mostly c's—you are successful at having relationships, are a valued friend, and generally are secure within yourself. You always think about your own viewpoint in the context of the wider picture and reap rewards from doing this.

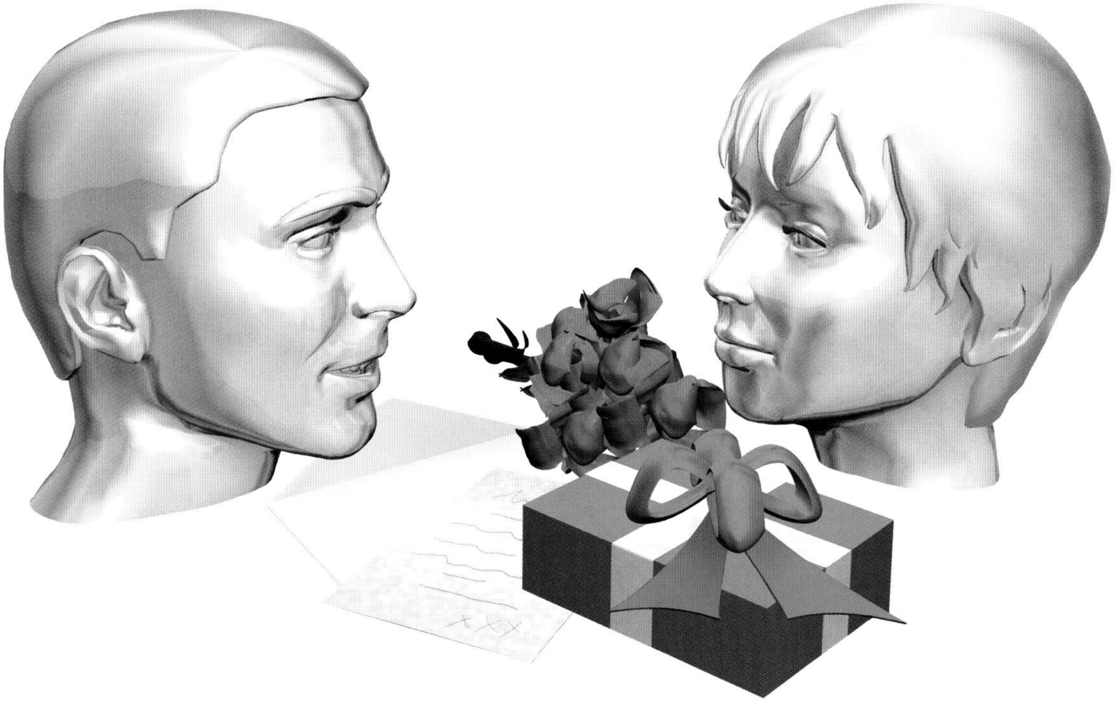

Do others influence your moods?

HAVE YOU EVER felt uplifted after hearing a motivational speaker or weepy after watching a sad movie? If so, then you've experienced a so-called "transfer of emotions," where you unknowingly imitate the emotions of others to re-create that mood within yourself. This effect is also mirrored in body language—if you are in tune with someone, you tend to copy each other's posture and mannerisms. The coordination of emotions and body language in this way is known as emotional rapport. It happens subconsciously, but emotionally intelligent people can learn to manipulate it. If you can influence someone's emotions, you can then connect with that person and be perceived as charismatic and emotionally attractive. Famous and infamous world leaders, like John F Kennedy, Winston Churchill, and Hitler elevated emotional rapport to a fine and, in some instances, destructive, art.

TEST YOURSELF

Test 1
You will need a pen and paper.

Firstly, make a list of the occasions when you tuned into someone else's mood. This might have been a friend who made you laugh when you were feeling down, or a movie that made you cry. Secondly, make a list of the times you succeeded in making others tune into your mood. This might have been a winning presentation that dazzled the audience, or cheering up a colleague with personal problems. Is it easier to convey your own mood, or to be in tune with another's?

Test 2
You will need a partner.

Ask your partner to imagine he or she had the best possible day at work, with an unexpected salary increase, public praise at a managers' meeting, and the go-ahead for a pet project. Now imagine you had the worst day at work: your assistant resigned, your boss undermined you in a meeting, and you missed out on a deserved promotion. Sit opposite each other and convey your good and bad moods respectively, verbally and non-verbally. Do you mirror each other's body language? Did you feel any emotional rapport? Whose mood was overriding by the end of the test?

Boosting tips

1. Study your friends' or colleagues' body language while you are talking to them. See if you can influence what they do next: cross your arms, or put your elbows on the table to see if they inadvertently copy your actions.

2. Watch the news or current affairs programs on TV. Notice how politicians and business leaders perform in front of an audience. What devices do they use to draw you in? How do different delivery styles accommodate the audience?

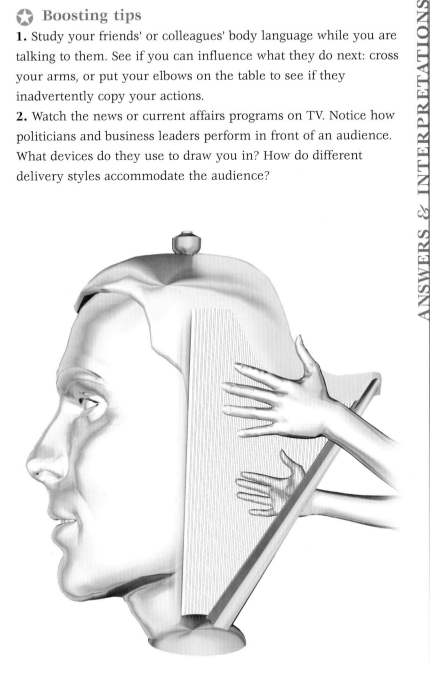

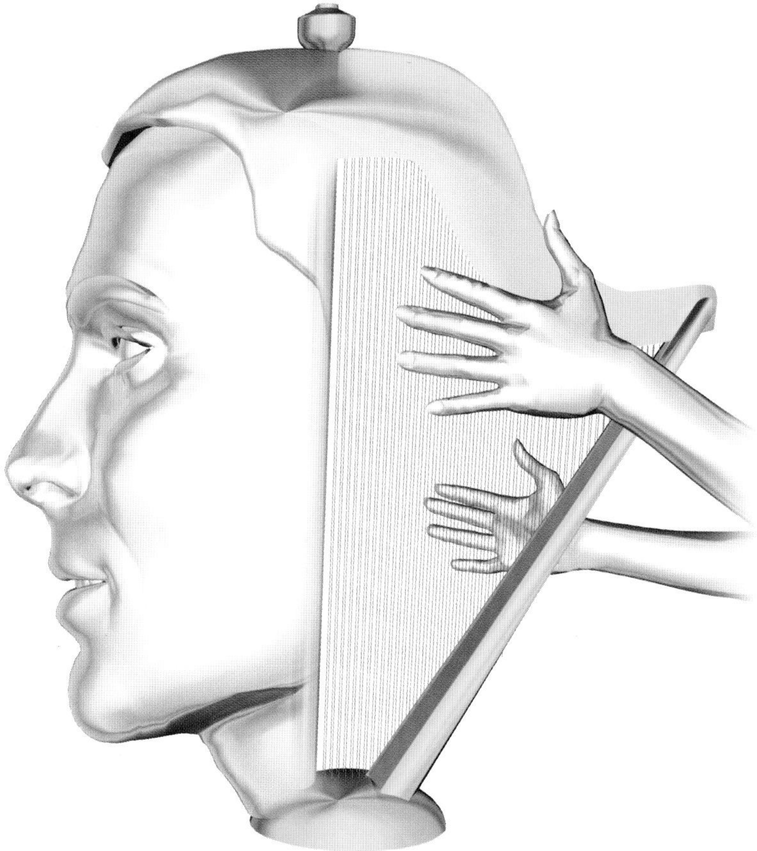

ANSWERS & INTERPRETATIONS

If you are able to tune into other people's moods, but are not influenced by them, you have average emotional rapport. Learn to feel the impact of other people's emotions by relating their experiences to events in your life that once evoked similar emotions.

If you are able to tune into other people's moods and are influenced by them, you have good emotional rapport. Influence other people's feelings by channeling your emotions and using raw, emotive language. It's hard to get an audience fired up if your heart is not in what you're saying.

If you are able to tune into other people's moods, are influenced by them, and can, in turn, influence the moods of others, you have excellent emotional rapport. This ability is vital in politics, business leadership, acting, and public speaking.

Are you a social person?

One of the more complex aspects of social intelligence, essential for forming new friendships, is the ability to integrate into different settings. Attending a partner's company function, joining a gym or a club, starting a new job, or chatting with strangers at a party, all involve blending into a group of people talking, sometimes as an outsider to a conversation. This type of social competence involves noticing, interpreting, and responding to quite subtle emotional and interpersonal cues.

It may be difficult to pinpoint what it is a popular person does right, but it's very obvious when someone gets it wrong. Being rejected or rebuffed by a group is very embarrassing, so we usually err on the side of caution. There are two tactics which guarantee rejection: trying to take the lead too soon, and not tuning into the sort of interactions that are going on. Interestingly, animals have exactly the same rules: a dominant male lion will see off any competition from another male attempting to lead.

TEST YOUR ABILITY

Imagine that you want to join a conversation at a party or a social gathering. You don't know any of the people who are standing and talking together in a group. Make a plan for joining in by ranking these actions, starting with the one you would do first. Put your first three actions into group a, your next three actions into group b, and your last four actions into group c.

1. Nod and smile to show non-verbal acceptance.
2. Wait until your acceptance is confirmed and/or your presence is acknowledged.
3. Change the subject.
4. Disagree with one or more group members.
5. Simply say "yes" or "ah!" to show mild verbal acceptance.
6. Observe the group.
7. Respond fully if asked a direct question.
8. Initiate conversation within the discussion topic.
9. Note the topic of discussion and the tone of the conversation.
10. Offer an opinion.

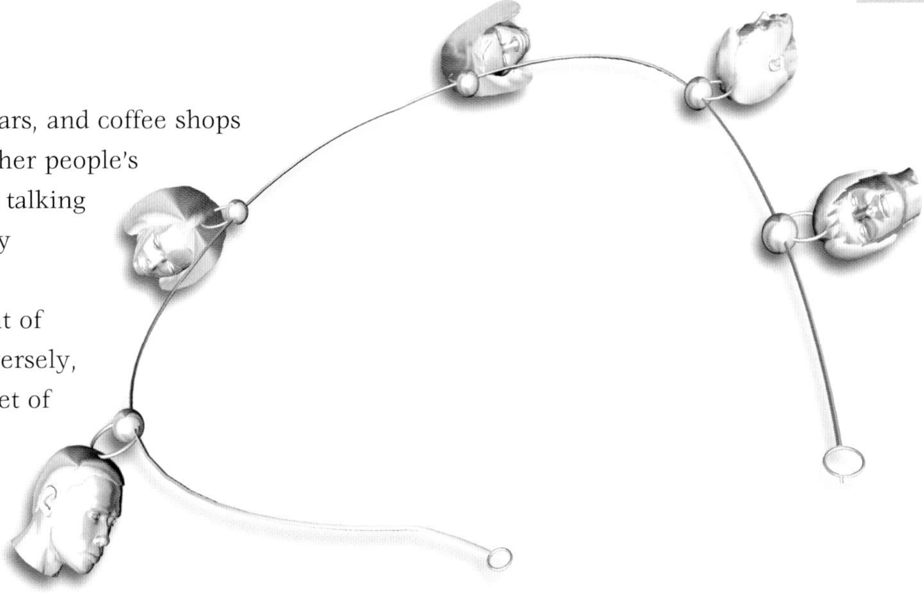

Boosting tips

1. Visit public places like restaurants, bars, and coffee shops with a notepad and a pen. Scrutinize other people's group dynamics: make a note of who is talking and who is listening. Jot down any body language and other non-verbal signals.

2. If you tend to eat alone, make a point of joining your colleagues for lunch. Conversely, if you habitually lunch with the same set of people, broaden your social abilities by sitting at a different table and inviting others to join you.

ANSWERS & INTERPRETATIONS

Although there will be differences depending on the type of situation, who is present, and your own confidence, the order of priorities should be:

Firstly, watch what's going on, observe the group dynamics (6), mentally taking note of the discussion topic and the tone of the conversation (9). Show non-verbal acceptance by nodding and smiling (1). Secondly, tentatively join in by showing mild verbal acceptance (saying simply "yes" or "ah!") (5). Wait to have your acceptance confirmed and/or your presence acknowledged positively (2). Respond promptly if directly asked a question (7). Thirdly, assert yourself very cautiously by initiating conversation within the discussion topic (8), and gently offering an opinion (10). Changing the subject (3), and disagreeing with one or more group members (4), are options for those already established in the group.

EXCELLENT

If you chose 6–9–1, then 5–2–7, then 8–10–3–4, IN THAT ORDER—you have excellent social emotional intelligence. You probably fit in easily wherever you go and enjoy meeting new people.

AVERAGE

If your choices for groups a, b, and c were 6–9–1, 5–2–7, and 8–10–3–4 respectively, but NOT in that exact order, or if you chose ANY other combination—you have average social emotional intelligence. You are likely to have a wide circle of friends, but attending a social event on your own, where you know few people, can make you feel nervous. Such situations really test our social skills—next time, take a friend to give you confidence, or rehearse conversation topics for small talk. If your body language is open and you look friendly and smile, you are a long way toward being approachable and approached.

Do you manage work relationships well?

Most people are aware of the importance of maintaining a good relationship with their manager and their co-workers. Relating well to people at work is an important part of being professionally successful. Developing good relations with colleagues should be one of your priorities, both in terms of productivity and personal advancement—horizontally (with fellow workers) and vertically (with managers and subordinates).

How much of your job involves networking with others, either inside and outside of your organization? The chances are this is a considerable part of your job. Networking and developing informal relationships with colleagues is often underestimated—it is the rare manager who recommends it as a growth opportunity or personal goal. Communication networks make the difference between getting a job done efficiently and quickly, and stumbling at hurdle after hurdle.

TEST YOURSELF

For each question, pick the TWO responses that best describe you.

1. A colleague comes to you for your advice. Is it usually:

a) A work issue requiring your experience.

b) A technical issue requiring your expertise.

c) A personal issue requiring your discretion.

2. You need a new software package installed on your computer, but it hasn't been budgeted for. Would you:

a) Plead with your boss about using an alternative budget.

b) Talk to your contact in IT about any installation requirements and ways of negotiating a deal with a supplier.

c) Conspire with a confidant about how to get round the system.

3. Can you think of someone at work who you would turn to if:

a) You wanted to find out who could help you from a particular department.

b) You needed specialist input for a project.

c) You were thinking of changing jobs.

4. You want your colleagues to help you celebrate your birthday. Would you invite:

a) A whole group who get along well together.

b) A few people who do a similar job to you.

Boosting tips

1. Take up any invitations to social events after work. Talk to people you meet at the drinks machine, the water cooler, or in the washroom. If you work in a large office, make it your mission to remember everyone you see regularly at work by name and be able to chat with everyone.

2. Volunteer for specialist training at work. Offer to help new staff by showing them the ropes.

c) One or two people whom you would class as close friends.

5. You have been asked to put together a project team to review working practices across the organization. Would you:

a) Call on your social contacts across the company.

b) Approach a select group of technical experts from the appropriate departments.

c) Ask your close work friends for their advice and opinions.

ANSWERS & INTERPRETATIONS

*Mainly a's indicate membership of a communications network.** You are part of a group of colleagues who talk regularly and have a warm social relationship. You can rely on each other to pull out the stops to get a job done. The best communication networks are cross-departmental.*

*Mainly b's indicate membership of an expertise network.** You have a reputation for technical excellence and, if you have a central role in this network, you are more likely to be promoted.*

*Mainly c's indicate membership of a trust network.** You belong to a tight-knit group, who exchange sensitive information like resentments or impending restructuring. You can rely on each other to be discrete and turn to each other in crises.*

Note your mix of responses (for example, mostly a's and c's, or an equal mix of all three). The real stars of an organization have multiple and stable connections in all three types of network. If you score highly for one network, try to develop relationships that represent the others.

* In *Emotional Intelligence: Why It Can Matter More Than IQ* (1995), Daniel Goleman describes three types of network—communications, expertise, and trust.

Are you a good negotiator?

THE TALENT TO mediate between warring parties, or to negotiate an advantageous position for yourself or your organization, is one of the more complex aspects of emotional intelligence. It requires the ability to recognize emotions in others, have empathy, and manage those emotions on behalf of other people. Great negotiators are in demand personally and professionally. They make excellent

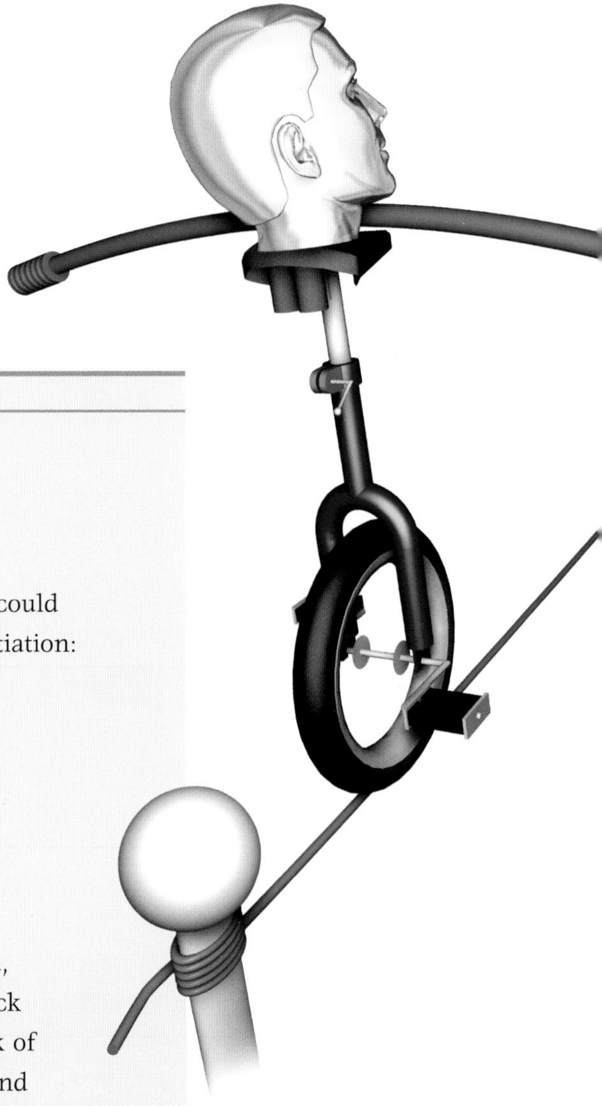

TEST YOURSELF

Test 1

You will need a pen and paper.

Write down as many ways as you can think of in which you could deliberately use the following emotions or feelings in a negotiation:

Excitement ***Anger*** ***Friendliness***

Test 2

You will need a pen and paper.

Imagine that you are involved in a negotiation, and that the other party completely loses his or her temper, shouts at you, and thumps the table with his or her fist. You could think back to a real-life example or simply envisage this situation. Think of the different ways in which you could address the outburst and diffuse the aggression.

diplomats, arbitrators, lawyers, estate agents, business tycoons, and members of the police force.

Practically every business interaction depends on some degree of negotiation: takeovers, job title changes, supplier contracts, even whose turn it is to go out for coffee and muffins. Professional negotiators excel at juggling extremes and judging how to best employ the points in between: they listen and talk, can argue the finer points, but manage to never lose sight of strategic considerations, knowing when to be flexible and when not to budge. Skilled negotiators can even save lives—their ability has succeeded in securing the release of hostages under terrifying conditions and against the odds, for example.

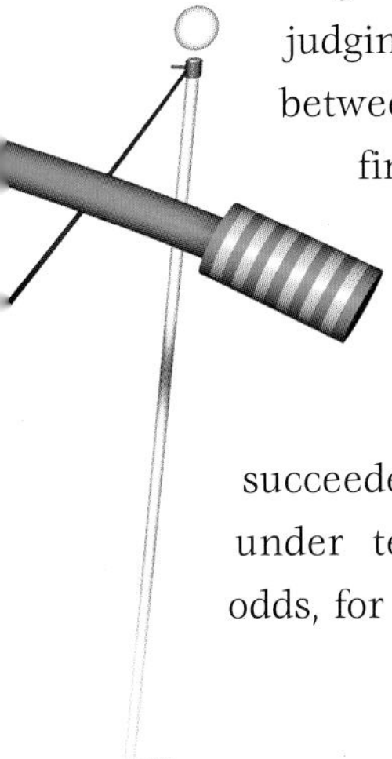

Boosting tips

1. Watch talented negotiators in action. Follow televised court cases and notice how attorneys concede on some points, but argue on others, and how they listen to evidence from the other side and then argue against its merits. Plea and sentence bargaining involves remarkable negotiation skills.

2. Listening is an essential skill for effective negotiating. Practice your listening skills by offering to take minutes at your next team meeting. This will force you to process what is being said as you write it down. If you don't understand a comment or decision, ask for clarification to avoid any misunderstandings.

ANSWERS & INTERPRETATIONS

TEST 1

You could use excitement to keep the momentum going. The other party will see it as an expression of commitment, enthusiasm, and energy. Anger should be used very carefully and in a controlled way. A short, sharp shock tells the other party that you are back in the driving seat if you feel you are being put upon. Friendliness is valuable during negotiations because it encourages the other party to relax, feel comfortable, and open up.

TEST 2

Stay calm. Be assertive and explicit about expressing your dislike of the current situation. Suggest time out. Resume the discussion on a calmer note.

If you thought of one use for the emotions in test 1, or two or less actions for test 2, you have average negotiating skills. The aim of negotiation is to remove obstacles to decisions, so your job is to find out what these obstacles are and why they exist. Keep going back until you have a position statement that you all agree on and then move forward.

If you thought of two uses for the emotions in test 1, or three actions for test 2, you have good negotiating skills. Keep your strategic intentions in mind, as well as an overview of the direction that the discussion is taking. Use visual prompts, displayed for both parties to view, if appropriate.

If you thought of three uses for the emotions in test 1, or four or more actions for test 2, you have excellent negotiating skills. This is an invaluable skill in mediating corporate mergers and acquisitions and pays dividends in private life, too.

Are you a good leader?

THE ROLE OF emotional intelligence in leadership is crucial: constructive criticism, feedback, and praise are all vital tools for improving staff motivation and performance. In *Primal Leadership: Realizing the Power of Emotional Intelligence* (2001), Daniel Goleman et al identify four positive approaches to leadership—visionary, coaching, affiliative, and democratic—and the fact that most successful leaders are able to switch between styles. Whether you're a team leader, department manager, or CEO, learning about your leadership style will lend you insight into the positive and negative aspects of your leadership potential.

Visionary leaders give clear directions, ensure everyone is working toward the organization's goals, but leave individuals free to decide how to best reach those targets. Coaching leaders connect what individuals want with the organization's objectives. Affiliative leaders develop close-knit and motivated teams by encouraging a healthy and friendly working environment almost above the organization's targets. Democratic leaders gain political support and commitment by encouraging participation. They make use of teamwork, negotiation, and empathy, so workers feel included, heard, and valued.

TEST YOURSELF

Put these statements in the order in which they apply to your beliefs about leadership.

1. I communicate my vision to my team, but it's down to them to innovate and experiment in order to achieve set goals.
2. I value people and their feelings, so I strive to keep them happy and to build up team spirit.
3. I believe that no single person has all the answers, so I frequently look to my team for ideas.
4. I believe in sharing information and knowledge so that everyone in the team feels included and is able to make a contribution.
5. I believe that if people are content and feel supported by their manager, the achievement of goals will follow.
6. I take the personal development of my staff very seriously.
7. I think that being a good listener is as important as being a good communicator.
8. I believe in my team, I invest in and care about individual members, so I expect the best effort from them.

ANSWERS & INTERPRETATIONS

If 1 and 4 were in your top 3 statements—you are a visionary type of leader. Try and combine this with an affiliative leadership style. A visionary leader may seem aloof and focused on the organization rather than the people, so being affiliative will sometimes counter this.

If 6 and 8 were in your top 3 statements—you are a coaching type of leader. Try and combine this approach with clear objectives and goals for team members that reflect the strategic direction of the organization.

If 2 and 5 were in your top 3 statements—you are an affiliative type of leader. Partner your style with the visionary approach. Caring for your employees is important, but they need to be given direction as well.

If 3 and 7 were in your top 3 statements—you are a democratic type of leader, and need to accept that there will be times when you will have to take charge and make autocratic decisions.

Boosting tips

1. Analyze any authority figures in your life in terms of their leadership style—your manager, your CEO, a religious leader, the current President.

2. Ask a group of people you have led, either in a social or professional setting, to take the test and evaluate your leadership style. Compare their results with your viewpoint.

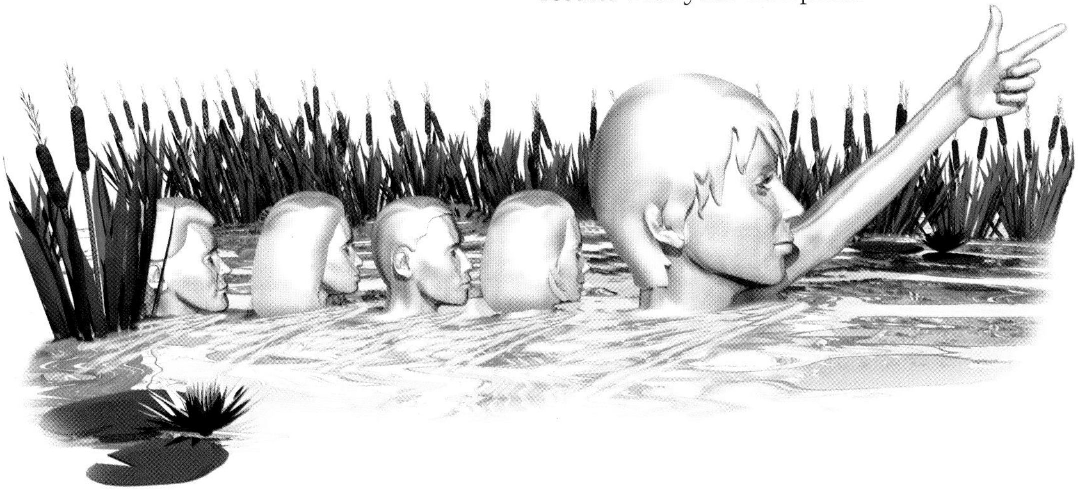

Your emotional intelligence

NOW THAT YOU'VE completed all the tests, you can profile your results to get an overall view of your strengths. Check the relevant boxes for each of your test profiles (*see opposite*).

- If you have 5 or more checks in the average column, you have adequate emotional intelligence. You are likely to enjoy the company of others, but find some emotional situations difficult or challenging.
- If you have 5 or more checks in the good column, or have an even spread of scores across all three categories, you have good emotional intelligence. You are likely to have a close support network, and only the occasional emotional flare-up.
- If you have 5 or more checks in the excellent column, you have superior emotional intelligence. You are likely to be popular, confident, and in a stable, loving relationship.

Developing and improving emotional intelligence

You have everything to gain from developing your emotional intelligence. Focus on improving empathy by trying to understand the motivations behind the behavior of others. Learn to resolve conflict by picking up good negotiation skills: effective listening is as important as effective talking. Develop your knowledge of group dynamics by watching and learning from socially skilled people in action.

Acting is a fun way of developing emotional intelligence because it asks you to pretend to be someone else, with a different perspective and set of motivations. Join an amateur drama society, or host a murder mystery party with friends, where you dress up as different characters and act out those parts.

If you possess adequate-to-good emotional intelligence, remember to consider what motivates others and put yourself in their shoes. Always look at the broader picture because everyone carries some emotional baggage.

If you have superior emotional intelligence, ask yourself whether your relationship with your parents or your children is everything you hoped for. Are you a talented manager or negotiator, but find your arguments with your partner frustrating or unfruitful? Put your core skills to better use in a more conscious and focused way.

Working with children

Emotional intelligence is a key skill for children to have and the benefits of getting on with your peers is a lifelong achievement. You could, for instance:

- Get your child to talk about his or her feelings when good and bad things happen to him or her. Every action has a motivation and behind every feeling is a thought. You may need to prompt him or her with questions like "How did you feel?" and "How do you think they felt?".
- Create opportunities and organize activities for social interaction for your child with his or her peer group outside of school. The ability to mix with people from all backgrounds is an essential life skill that will serve your child well in later years.

PARTNER RELATIONSHIPS			
	Average ✓	*Good ✓*	*Excellent ✓*
Test 1 (pages 82-83)			
	Avoidance	*Volatile*	*Resolution*
Test 2 (pages 84-85)			
FAMILY RELATIONSHIPS			
	Not close	*Close*	*Very close*
Test 1 (pages 88-89)			
	Aquaintance	*Family*	*Friend*
Test 2 (pages 90-91)			
	Average ✓	*Good ✓*	*Excellent ✓*
Test 3 (pages 92-93)			
SOCIAL RELATIONSHIPS			
	Average ✓	*Good ✓*	*Excellent ✓*
Test 1 (pages 94-95)			
	Managing emotions	*Building empathy*	*Handling emotions in others*
Test 2 (pages 96-97)			
	Average ✓	*Good ✓*	*Excellent ✓*
Test 3 (pages 98-99)			
PROFESSIONAL RELATIONSHIPS			
	One network	*Two networks*	*All three networks*
Test 1 (pages 100-01)			
	Average ✓	*Good ✓*	*Excellent ✓*
Test 2 (pages 102-03)			
	Affiliative or democratic	*Coaching*	*Visionary*
Test 3 (pages 104-05)			

5

PERSONAL

INTELLIGENCE

What is personal intelligence?

Personal intelligence is our capacity to self-manage through knowing, recognizing, and understanding our feelings, desires, and intentions. Without it, we are awash with turbulent emotions, buffeted about like a rudderless boat on stormy seas, prone to irrational outbursts and moody withdrawals. With it, we are able to motivate ourselves, can delay impulsive reactions to stressful situations and learn to take control.

At first glance, our emotions would seem to be readily accessible: we know when we are angry and when we feel happy. However, there are times when we behave in a certain way because of feelings that lie beneath the surface, occasions when a comment like "You're in a bad mood!" takes us by surprise. This usually prompts an internal process of examination and recognition of why this is, perhaps the rude reaction of a shop assistant earlier on that day or the arrival of a hefty bill in the mail. The capacity to mentally review thoughts and feelings prior to initiating actions embodies true personal intelligence.

Internal emotions

Emotions are psychological and physical responses to feelings. Some are straightforward such as sadness, happiness, and fear, although many subtle nuances exist within each of these. Others are complex blends of emotions like jealousy—a combination of anger, sadness, fear, and anxiety. Similarly, love can be a mixture of happiness, pride, security, and comfort. An appreciation of the range and variety of emotions that impact on our moods and thoughts, is the first step toward personal intelligence.

Self-awareness

The ability to continually monitor internal thinking by stepping back and questioning thoughts and feelings as if one were looking in from the outside is known as self-awareness. All too often, faulty thinking inhibits us and phrases like "I don't want to think about that," or "I shouldn't have spoken up" pop into our heads. Self-awareness ought to be a constructive process but we are often harsh critics or overly judgmental. Allowing events to be reframed positively takes time and a cool head.

Self-management

There is a significant gap between feeling something and acting on it. Strong self-management is required to pull the two apart. If you are feeling down, for example, it makes sense to want to cheer yourself up and the ability to turn a mood around is a vital life skill. Although basic emotional self-control is learned from a very young age—toddlers, for example, are taught not to demand the impossible or to shout and cry when thwarted—the ability to control complex emotions challenges even the most emotionally intelligent among us.

Why is personal intelligence important?

It is difficult to think of an aspect of life that does not benefit from having highly developed personal intelligence. Instead of being prey to a negative emotion, you will be able to think through why you are feeling this way, consider whether there is a "real" reason behind this sensation, and work through the options for change. Such in-depth analysis has the knock-on effect of giving you insight into other people's emotions and actions. You can then use this knowledge to change how you view or deal with others. As a result, you are more likely to be positive, happy, optimistic, and mentally resilient.

When you use personal intelligence at work, you will gain a reputation as someone who is able to keep a team together, and doesn't create conflict, but can manage it when it occurs. Optimism goes hand-in-hand with enthusiasm and positive energy, which keeps an organization dynamic and forward-moving. You will be popular with colleagues and valued for your honesty and support. Office politics is a part of daily living, but you will have the necessary skills to recognize power games and sail through unscathed. As a result, you are more likely to be productive, promoted, trusted, and better equipped at handling stress.

People with high personal intelligence are insightful, in control, in harmony with themselves and those around them. They tend to envisage optimistic outcomes, which they then make happen by maintaining a positive mindset.

Are you self-aware?

THE CORNERSTONE of emotional intelligence is being aware of feelings as they occur. The next foundation block is deciding to change those feelings for the better. This can involve drawing on inner resources from deep within and may require considerable emotional strength. People with this ability are usually psychologically healthy and have a positive outlook on life.

Self-awareness doesn't mean lengthy ruminations about negative emotions. Once a disturbing emotion has been identified, individuals with high personal intelligence will not dwell on it and seek to snap out of it. It may seem contradictory that self-aware people look outwardly, not inwardly, but being able to reframe negative emotions often needs an informed perception of other people's feelings and viewpoints.

TEST YOURSELF

Check the four statements below that most apply to you.

☐ **1.** I am usually in a good mood—that's just the way I am.

☐ **2.** When I'm in a bad mood, I can usually reverse it by thinking positively.

☐ **3.** Sometimes I can't explain why I'm feeling particularly happy or sad.

☐ **4.** If something terrible happens in the world, I try not to think about it because it can be too upsetting.

☐ **5.** If I feel irritable, I stop and ask myself why.

☐ **6.** I sometimes feel overwhelmed by my emotions and emotionally out of control.

☐ **7.** I constantly notice my emotions, pausing to reflect on why they arose and whether I want to change them.

☐ **8.** I find it very difficult to change my mood if I'm depressed.

Boosting tips

1. Keep a notepad and jot down every emotion that you feel in the course of one day no matter how fleeting or superficial. Before you go to bed, make a note of how long every emotion lasted and whether you took any action to change it.

2. Buy a "bad mood" basket (for when you're feeling down) and fill it up with your favorite things, which you can then retrieve when you need to lift yourself up emotionally.

☐ **9.** When someone seems to have it in for me, I make a concerted effort to think about things from their perspective.

☐ **10.** Sometimes I know I should try to buck up when feeling low, but I don't have the energy.

ANSWERS & INTERPRETATIONS

Total the number of points for the four statements that were most applicable to you.

1. 5 points; 2. 10 points; 3. 2 points; 4. 5 points; 5. 10 points; 6. 2 points; 7. 10 points; 8. 2 points; 9. 10 points; 10. 5 points

20 points or less—you have an engulfed self-awareness style.* Because you are unable to analyze your feelings naturally, you should make a concerted effort to pinpoint your emotions. As they may sometimes seem overwhelming, you can feel out of control. Learn to take responsibility for what you are feeling.

Between 20 and 30 points—you have an accepting self-awareness style*, are conscious of your feelings and moods, but you let them wash over you without trying to change them. The time has come for you to move on and put things right.

30 points or over—you have a self-aware style.* You are able to monitor and manage your feelings and moods, and take steps to redress negative emotions. Take time to examine and consider other people's feelings as psychological insight into the motivation of those around you is very valuable.

* **In *Emotional Intelligence: Why It Can Matter More Than IQ* (1995),Daniel Goleman describes three emotional self-awareness styles (engulfed, accepting, and self-aware).**

Are you afraid of being alone?

OVERCOMING the fear of solitude is important for effective emotional self-awareness. It gives you an opportunity to take stock and learn to love yourself. We all rely on others for companionship to some extent, but total dependency is unhealthy. If you start to truly enjoy time on your own, you will embark on a process of self-discovery: you will value yourself more, you'll come to know yourself better, and you will acquire deeper insights into your strengths and weaknesses.

Do you look forward to your own company and thrive on isolation, or feel anxious and uncomfortable at the mere thought of being left alone? If you enjoy being by yourself, chances are you're introverted and obtain your energy from within. If you loathe the idea of solitude, you are more likely to be extroverted and get your energy from those around you. Introverts actually need to be on their own to recharge their mental batteries as they find having to interact with other people draining. Extroverts find being on their own depressing; it makes them feel lonely and they don't see their own company as valuable.

Keeping a personal diary is an excellent technique for getting to know yourself as it provides a vehicle for contemplation. In it, you can be completely honest in a way that is impossible with others around you. Get to know yourself better by dedicating time from your hectic schedule to make this a priority.

TEST YOURSELF

Try writing a daily journal for one week. Find a time and a place—like before going to bed—where you won't be interrupted. Write for at least 15 minutes, either on paper or on a keyboard, about yourself and your relationships.

Don't worry about spelling or grammar. Allow your mind to roam: write about something you are worried about, something you would love to happen, how you feel, who you love, even questions that you want answered.

ANSWERS & INTERPRETATIONS

If you were uncomfortable dwelling on yourself, found it difficult to set aside time, or gave up diary writing within the week—you have an average solitude comfort zone. You enjoy being with people and find time on your own to be quite lonely.

If you enjoyed getting worries off your chest, set aside time without too much effort, but found your enthusiasm waned— you have a good solitude comfort zone. You enjoy outside company, but need occasional time on your own to recharge.

If you were hooked on self-reflecting, are still keeping a diary, and enjoyed discovering things about yourself—you have an excellent solitude comfort zone. You probably have deep inner resources and can cope with any situation.

Boosting tips

1. Go on dates with yourself: try having dinner alone in a restaurant or go to a movie on your own. Repeat these occasions until you stop feeling self-conscious.

2. Find a quiet, secluded spot in the park where you can sit for 10 minutes. Practice breathing in and out slowly and deeply. Focus on a nearby object like a tree or a cloud and let your thoughts wander.

Can you distinguish between thoughts, emotions, and reactions?

DISTINGUISHNG BETWEEN thoughts, emotions, and reactions is difficult to do because they occur almost simultaneously as prompted by external factors. One of the main obstacles to recognizing thoughts accurately is faulty or self-defeatist deduction in the form of "She shouted at me so she must hate me." Such thinking takes things too personally, overgeneralizes, and focuses on the bad. The ability to separate and classify thoughts as cognitive processes, emotions as psychological outcomes, and reactions as physical responses, is key to highly developed and effective self-awareness.

TEST YOURSELF

Categorize the following options as a thought, an emotion, or a reaction.

1. You spend an hour getting ready for your partner's company party, but he forgets to compliment you on your appearance. Would you:

a) Wish he would comment on it.
b) Ask him how you look.
c) Feel dejected he hasn't noticed the extra effort you've put in.

2. Your mother sends you a beautiful gift to congratulate you on your promotion. Would you:

a) Appreciate the gesture.
b) Be really pleased she's proud of you.
c) Phone her to say thank you.

3. Your best friend cancels lunch with you at the last minute for a hot new date. Would you:

a) Be upset.
b) Believe her loyalties are misplaced.
c) Not give it much importance and rearrange your lunch engagement.

4. You've just started a new job and a colleague in the office is undermining you in front of your manager. Would you:

a) Privately set the record straight with your boss.
b) Feel annoyed at your colleague's deviousness.
c) Wonder why your colleague feels threatened by you.

Boosting tips

1. Write down some thought = > feeling = > action sequences to "what if" scenarios. For example, what if your partner came home very late from work and hadn't called you? What if you lost your job?

2. Ask a friend for his or her point of view on an argument you both had a long time ago. You may find that he or she has a completely different perspective on it than you.

5. On a night out, a couple of your friends have an argument and storm out. Would you:

a) Experience annoyance at the fact they have ruined the evening.

b) Decide not to get involved.

c) Rather they forget their differences and move on.

ANSWERS & INTERPRETATIONS

Score 1 point for each correct response
Maximum score = 15

1. a) thought; b) reaction; c) emotion
2. a) thought; b) emotion; c) reaction
3. a) emotion; b) thought; c) reaction
4. a) reaction; b) emotion; c) thought
5. a) emotion; b) reaction; c) thought

6 points or less—you have average self-awareness, and are likely to be an emotional person who acts and speaks first, and only thinks afterward. Because you tend to be direct, you are not perceived as calculating or devious, but are not always in control. Notice the difference between reactions and actions: you decide to take action, but a reaction "happens" to you. Aim to take control and act, rather than react.

Between 7 and 13 points—you have good self-awareness, and probably find it hard to see the subtle differences between thoughts and feelings, but can exercise self-control when it comes to acting and reacting. Feelings are difficult to hold back once the floodgates have been opened, so remember to go back to your thoughts and be tough and realistic with yourself.

14 points or more—you have excellent self-awareness, are able to exercise control over your feelings, and can prevent inappropriate emotional outbursts. This ability is invaluable in highly charged occupations like the emergency services.

Do you express or repress emotions?

We use the range of information available from our senses, thoughts, past experiences, and emotions to make decisions, both large and small. There is a strong correlation between events and feelings: a sense of loss makes you feel sad or a current event can dig up past emotions. Feelings are an important part of us, but we have choices about how best to deal with them. Typically, you can either vent your feelings, or suppress and keep them to yourself. Do you often fly off the handle? Do you feel tearful whenever anything goes wrong? Do you find it hard to get worked up about anything or do you feel numb even when you should be furious? By learning to effectively respond to your feelings, you can find additional ways for emotional self-expression.

Any occasion in which your behavior is influenced, or can potentially be influenced, by a feeling grants you an opportunity to exert some form of decision-making about the intensity of, and the way in which you wish to express a particular emotion.

TEST YOURSELF

You will need a pen and paper. Think back to a life event that you found upsetting at the time like a relationship finishing or a permanent break-up with a close friend.

- Did the strength of your feelings correspond to the situation?
- Did you have conflicting emotions?
- Did you have any preconceptions or biases that impacted on the way you then felt?
- What judgments did you make about the event?

How would you respond if you found yourself in the same situation today? Write down your ideas, asking yourself:

- What are my options for expressing my feelings?
- What would be the consequences of each option for me?
- What would be the consequences of each option for the other person involved?
- What result am I hoping for?
- What do I want to do?
- What would happen if I did nothing?

Boosting tips

1. Write down a list of imaginary occasions when repressing your emotions would be appropriate.

2. Draw a decision tree based on expressing and repressing your emotions for the same root issue, and branch out the likely scenarios depending on the emotional choices that you make. If you feel that your boss isn't supporting you, you could a) tell him or her how you feel; b) moan to a colleague; c) put up with it and look for another job. If you choose a), you could plan a meeting and prepare evidence to support your emotional upset, or you could burst into her office and slam the door. If you choose to set up a meeting, you are more likely (although not certain) to achieve emotional balance and the outcome that you seek.

ANSWERS & INTERPRETATIONS

If your responses allowed you to postpone or avoid painful feelings by repressing your emotions, you have average emotional self-management. For example, if a close friend is moving away, you might avoid him or her so as not to have to say goodbye. Remember that you have lots of options available when it comes to expressing an emotion—you don't have to choose between extremes.

If your responses allowed you to acknowledge your emotions, you have good emotional self-management. For example, if a close friend is moving away, you might choose to spend more time with him or her before the person leaves. Ask yourself some probing questions to gain insight. What is this emotion that I am feeling? What is it telling me about the situation? Why am I feeling it at this particular time? When and why have I felt this way before?

If your responses gave you the opportunity to express your emotions, even though it was painful, you have excellent emotional self-management. For example, if a close friend is moving away, you might choose to arrange a weekend away together in a few month's time so you can catch up with him or her.

Are you an optimist or a pessimist?

Optimists see failure as temporary, non-personal, and specific, due to reasons that can be altered. They might think, "That didn't go well today, but I learned a lot from it and will improve." Pessimists see failure as permanent, personal, and part of life, attributable to reasons they cannot change. They might think, "That didn't go well because I just can't seem to get it right." Surprisingly, optimism and pessimism are learned behaviors, not an inherent and unchangeable part of our personalities. Optimism is a crucial part of emotional intelligence—it enables you to bounce back from failure or disaster and learn from it. Optimists outperform all others in life: they have a positive frame of reference, come up with more solutions to problems, don't dwell on bad experiences, and believe good things will come their way (and generally they do). It is worth noting, however, that true optimism is realistic and not deluded or naïve.

TEST YOURSELF

Which of these two options best describe you?

1. *If I am late in finishing a report at work, I am more likely to think that:*
a) My time management was poor and I had too many interruptions.
b) I'll have to schedule more time next time.

2. *If I tell a joke at a dinner party and everyone laughs, I am likely to think that:*
a) It's a hilarious joke.
b) I was on good form and my comic timing was impeccable.

3. *If my boss shouts at me, I am likely to think that:*
a) He must be irritated because I've done something wrong.
b) He's just in a bad mood.

4. *If I failed to get elected to my staff committee at work, I am more likely to think that:*
a) People didn't like my ideas.
b) I didn't communicate my ideas well enough.

5. *When I succeed at something, this is more likely to:*
a) Make me feel pleased at having managed to avoid the potential pitfalls.
b) Inspire me to stretch myself even further.

ANSWERS & INTERPRETATIONS

Mostly a's—you tend to be more pessimistic than optimistic and probably believe in fate. You come to expect personal criticism and may see yourself in the role of the victim.

Equal mix of a's and b's—you are equally pessimistic and optimistic, and probably see yourself as quite upbeat, but with a tendency to doom and gloom if you let your guard down.

Mostly b's—you are extremely optimistic and emotionally robust. You would excel in a sales environment, where optimism buffers against rejection.

Boosting tips

1. List five events in the past week that were directly influenced by your optimism or pessimism. For each one, write down the separate thought processes and the likely outcome depending on whether you were being optimistic or pessimistic.

2. Think about the characters in a book that you are currently reading. Define each one either as an optimist or a pessimist, or a mixture of both. Identify the personality traits in each of these characters that made you come to your conclusions.

Can you change your mood?

MOODS ARE prolonged extensions of emotions resulting from a trigger event or a chain of events. Emotions are usually quite strong feelings, that exist in the heat of the moment, whereas moods are more low-key and can last for hours or even days. Emotionally intelligent people recognize when a mood starts to fade and take the necessary steps to pull themselves back out again. Bad, or depressive, moods create faulty thinking that is limited (and limiting) in scope, cause negative thoughts, and block mental agility. The ability to lift your mood, or change it for the better, is essential for your mental health and emotional success whatever age you are.

TEST YOURSELF

Imagine you feel depressed and in low spirits. Check the four coping mechanisms that would most apply to you.

☐ **1.** I have a good cry.

☐ **2.** I find something to distract me like watching an exciting sporting event or a comedy.

☐ **3.** I go out for a brisk walk, or head off to the gym.

☐ **4.** I go window shopping or treat myself to something at the mall.

☐ **5.** I always remember to compare myself to someone who is worse off.

☐ **6.** Soak in a soothing hot bath with scented candles and essential oils.

☐ **7.** I have an alcoholic drink.

☐ **8.** I buy my favorite food, order a take-out, or cook myself a special meal.

☐ **9.** I take the day off work and stay in bed.

☐ **10.** I tackle a household chore that I've been putting off for ages.

ANSWERS & INTERPRETATIONS

Total the number of points for the four coping mechanisms that were most applicable to you.

1. 5 points; 2. 10 points; 3. 10 points;
4. 5 points; 5. 5 points; 6. 5 points;
7. 2 points; 8. 2 points; 9. 2 points;
10. 10 points

Under 15 points—you have average mood-lifting abilities, and are likely to find moods fairly difficult to shift. Remember to count your blessings; think of all that has gone right for you; enjoy your life with friends and people who care about you.

Between 15 and 25 points—you have good mood-lifting abilities, and are more likely to be able to recognize a mood and take steps to change it. Discover what triggers bad feelings and prompts foul moods. Start reducing, avoiding, and eliminating such things: don't watch weepy movies, keep a distance from other people's bad moods, limit any stressful activities. Don't fret about insignificant things.

Over 25 points—you have excellent mood-lifting abilities, and are more likely to be a positive person with the inner resources to improve your mood. You would excel in the medical services, where people need to deal with distressing situations, but not let their work depress them.

Boosting tips

1. Be kind to yourself after a hard day. Have a facial, use aromatherapy oils, rent your favorite movie, go dancing, or bury your nose in a book you've been meaning to read.

2. Become more active—take a walk around the block every lunchtime, or get off the bus a couple of stops early. Exercise produces endorphins, your body's natural "happy" drug.

Do you have a "healthy" head?

It is natural to feel a range of emotions and moods. Most people are able to bounce back from anxious and depressive thoughts, reactions to stressful situations, or difficult life events. However, if mental depressive symptoms develop and these feelings persist, they start to interfere with a person's normal functioning. People who are depressed lose their sparkle and enjoyment of life. They struggle to sleep, concentrate, and feel motivated. Although we have all felt a bit down from time to time, the ability to shake off depressing feelings is critical for keeping a "healthy" head. We have also all felt anxious at significant points in our lives: before a job interview perhaps, or a presentation to the board. Such feelings of anxiety amount to the body producing an extreme physiological reaction in response to a perceived threat. Once the "threat" subsides, so should the symptoms, but they can sometimes continue, resulting in an avoidance of specific trigger situations. Phobias are fairly common types of anxieties. They represent an irrational fear of certain objects, animals, or places, like arachnophobia (an aversion to spiders) or claustrophobia (a terror of confined spaces). Panic attacks are another common anxiety symptom.

TEST YOURSELF

Answer these questions either with a "yes" or a "no" response.

Have you ever:

1. Taken extreme measures to avoid certain places or situations?
2. Felt your heart race and got hot flushes?
3. Felt so sad that you couldn't face anyone or anything?
4. Had sudden and intense feelings of impending doom or fear?
5. Fixed your mind on something and not been able to stop worrying about it?
6. Had a terrible fear of something, which others thought was out of proportion?
7. Felt that you were going to die and had palpitations, faintness, and sweating?
8. Felt low and couldn't seem to shake it off?

ANSWERS & INTERPRETATIONS

If you answered "yes" to questions 2 and 5, you have had general anxiety symptoms, and probably worry considerably about what other people think. Ensure your anxiety is not taking over your life.

If you answered "yes" to questions 1 and 6, you have had phobic symptoms, and may be able to avoid their cause, but should investigate tackling the trigger head-on.

If you answered "yes" to questions 4 and 7, you have had panic attack symptoms, and would benefit from learning to control your breathing patterns. Overly shallow or deep breathing is at the root of many panic attack symptoms.

If you answered "yes" to questions 3 and 8, you have had depressive symptoms. You may have had a difficult time in the past, and need to address the reasons for these feelings.

If you answered "no" to all the questions, you have a "healthy" head and are able to manage any anxious or depressing thoughts before they take root. If you answered "yes" to most of the questions, you could benefit from professional support and should consult your doctor.

Boosting tips

1. If you suffer from phobias, make an appointment with a cognitive behavioral therapist, who can help you retrain your thinking and tease out the reasons behind any anxious or distressing thoughts.

2. To keep a sense of perspective when you are feeling low, set yourself small but achievable goals during the day like cooking a meal or taking a walk.

3. Buy a relaxation tape. Set time aside in which to unwind, using it to learn to relax and regulate your breathing. This will help you to maintain a healthy head and avoid letting things get on top of you.

4. To combat depression, make sure you exercise regularly, maintain a healthy diet, and keep in touch with friends.

Can you help yourself think straight?

YOU'RE PROBABLY barely aware of the inner dialogue going on inside of you, those private thoughts that pass through your head. They are useful for assessing progress, development, and improvement within yourself. If unchecked, they can be psychologically corrosive and undermine your chances of success. You do not have to accept self-talk as gospel—the ability to monitor and challenge these thoughts is part of good personal intelligence. You don't have to believe such thoughts; try to call on yourself to find evidence to support them.

Everyone uses distorted or faulty thinking at some point in their lives: who, for example, hasn't ever used words like "I should," "I ought," or "I have to?" There are three main types of faulty thinking: all-or-nothing, when things are either great or terrible; I-feel-therefore-I-am, when feeling something is deemed the same as being it ("I feel stupid so I must be stupid"); and mind reading, assuming you know what someone else is really thinking ("I know she thinks I'm boring"). Learn your own pitfalls and start to love and defend yourself from within.

TEST YOURSELF

You will need a pen and paper. Draw a four-column table on a large piece of paper. Head the columns "event," "emotions," "thoughts," and "challenge to thoughts" **(see opposite for an example).** ***Complete this table using two key emotional events in your life in the past few months that have really upset you or made you mad. Challenging your thoughts can be difficult, so here are some self-examination questions to get you started.***

- I want him to love me. (How do you know he doesn't?)
- I'm angry. (Who with? About what?)
- My mother doesn't understand me. (What specifically doesn't she understand? How do you know?)
- I feel stupid. (Why? How? Compared to whom?)
- It's impossible to talk to my manager. (What would happen if you did? What is stopping you?)

Boosting tip

Pick one of your distorted assumptions and try to prove yourself wrong. If you feel you haven't been a good friend, for example, look for evidence to prove yourself wrong, and plan some activities or quality time with your friend.

ANSWERS & INTERPRETATIONS

If you were able to challenge most of your negative thoughts, but found it difficult to view them from a detached perspective, you have average positive self-talk. Try to be more aware of your inner dialogue and remember that what you think isn't always true.

If you were able to challenge every thought constructively, and reframe your thinking rationally, you have good positive self-talk. Now that you know how to confront distorted thoughts, ensure you keep up the good work.

If you seldom have negative thoughts and generally try to think the best of yourself and others, you have excellent positive self-talk. You have trained inner dialogue to think positively and realistically about highly charged emotional situations.

Event	*Emotions*	*Thoughts*	*Challenge to thoughts*
• A friend leaves you a phone message to cancel lunch at the last minute.	• Hurt, sad, annoyed	• She had a better offer. • She doesn't really value our friendship. • I'm not good company.	• She's never canceled before and must have had a good reason. • She's always remembered important dates like my birthday.

What is your natural temperament?

After exploring feelings and moods, psychologists discovered temperament to be our deepest emotional trait, reflecting those moods most prevalent in an individual. It also provides a backdrop to emotions, and influences the way we interpret events and our responses to them. It is something we are born with: ask any mother about her baby's temperament and she will describe it accurately and in detail.

Hippocrates, the father of Greek medicine, categorized temperament into fire, air, earth, and water. Western medicine refined this concept further into choleric (fire: impulsive, excitable, energetic); sanguine (air: outgoing, easygoing, adaptable); melancholic (earth: reserved, thoughtful, sober); and phlegmatic (water: careful, passive, even-tempered).

Jerome Kagan, a psychologist at Harvard University, recently gave temperament research a neuropsychological twist by proposing four "new" temperament types—upbeat, bold, melancholy, and timid. Each temperament type is apparently defined by a different brain activity and temperament can be subtly altered—not all timid babies, for example, grow up into shy adults. Armed with a highly developed personal intelligence, adaptable parenting styles can mold and help children to confidently face the world.

TEST YOURSELF

From the options below, pick the THREE statements that most apply to you.

1. I am not intimidated by talking to strangers and people in authority.
2. If I don't know people well, I won't say much, even if someone directly speaks to me.
3. I think the world is a difficult and dangerous place to live in.
4. I can find something to enjoy in most things.
5. I was a shy child.
6. I am generally good-humored and sociable.
7. I find it difficult to bounce back after a major initial setback.
8. I love trying out things I've never done before.

ANSWERS & INTERPRETATIONS

If 2 and 5 were in your top 3 statements—your temperament is timid, your element is water, and your humor is phlegmatic. Your strengths are your carefulness, calm, and perseverance. Your weaknesses are your shyness and your dislike of change.

If 1 and 8 were in your top 3 statements—your temperament is bold, your element is air, and your humor is sanguine. Your strengths are your sociability, eloquence, and friendliness. Your weaknesses are your lack of attention to detail and your impatience.

If 4 and 6 were in your top 3 statements—your temperament is upbeat, your element is fire, and your humor is choleric. Your strengths are your energy, stamina, and extroversion. Your weaknesses are your intolerance and forcefulness.

If 3 and 7 were in your top 3 statements—your temperament is melancholy, your element is earth, and your humor is melancholic. Your strengths are your intellect, thoughtfulness, and powers of observation. Your weaknesses are your pessimism and reserve.

Boosting tips

1. Think of occupations whose job characteristics fit each of the four temperament types. Remember to consider situations where apparently "bad" traits can be advantageous. For example, a child who dislikes change may be less influenced by peer pressure and, as an adult, become the perfect candidate for a role with strong guidelines and regulations such as the military or the world of business.

2. Ask your parents or grandparents to describe your temperament when you were a baby. How do their impressions compare with your view of yourself as an adult? Ask them how they think you have changed.

Your personal intelligence

NOW THAT YOU'VE completed all the tests, you can profile your results to get an overall view of your strengths. Check the relevant boxes for each of your test scores.

- If you have 5 or more checks in the average column, you have adequate personal intelligence. Your heart probably has the upper hand. This means you are likely to recognize your feelings, but find it difficult to rationalize and keep them under control.
- If you have 5 or more checks in the good column, or have an even spread of scores across all three categories, you have good personal intelligence. Your head and heart generally work in harmony, but sometimes your heart takes precedence. You are likely to have good self-awareness but occasionally react, rather than plan, the right course of action.
- If you have 5 or more checks in the excellent column, you have superior personal intelligence. Your head and heart complement each other. You are likely to be happy, successful, and in good mental shape.

Make a note of your temperament from your answers to internal emotions tests one and three.

Developing and improving personal intelligence

Learning and developing personal intelligence starts in infancy and should continue throughout life. What are you feeling? Why are you feeling it? Think about your feelings to try and identify the root cause, and keep delving back until you reach the source. If, as is usually the case, someone else is involved, put yourself in his or her shoes. What is he or she feeling? Why is he or she feeling that way? This is perhaps the most difficult emotional skill to acquire, but one that is essential for personal growth.

What could you do to make yourself feel better?

- Use the emotional charge from feelings of anger to feel energized, not livid.
- Recognize that you have choices about how you act. Consider in advance how you would feel with each decision taken and what the result would be.

If you have adequate-to-good personal intelligence, you already know that understanding your emotions will benefit all areas of your life, but sometimes it's hard to think rationally in the heat of the moment. Try to create a space between what you feel and what you do about it. Take time out, even a couple of minutes, if you feel you are losing control. Your aim should be to act, rather than react.

If you have superior personal intelligence, make sure you apply your self-knowledge to your relationships with others because not everyone is gifted in personal intelligence. There will always be people with whom you have to work or socialize who will not have your degree of insight, so be generous and in control on their behalf. Remember it takes two to have an argument.

Working with children

Born with little self-awareness, children gradually come to realize that not everything revolves around them. Self-control and the realization of choice in how they act are key lessons. You can encourage this by:

- Talking about what triggers emotions, particularly anger. Examine the more positive outlets of rage: assertiveness, for example, is a key emotional skill to have in order to counter the negative aspects of wrath.

Self-awareness			
	Engulfed	*Accepting*	*Self-aware*
***Test 1* (pages 112-13)**			
	Average ✓	*Good ✓*	*Excellent ✓*
***Test 2* (pages 114-15)**			
***Test 3* (pages 116-17)**			
Self-management			
	Average ✓	*Good ✓*	*Excellent ✓*
***Test 1* (pages 118-19)**			
	Pessimistic	*Combination of both*	*Optimistic*
***Test 2* (pages 120-21)**			
	Average ✓	*Good ✓*	*Excellent ✓*
***Test 3* (pages 122-23)**			
Internal emotions			
	Phobic/depressed/ panic attacks	*General anxiety*	*"Healthy" head*
***Test 1* (pages 124-25)**			
	Average ✓	*Good ✓*	*Excellent ✓*
***Test 2* (pages 126-27)**			
***Test 3* (pages 128-29)**			

6

PHYSICAL

INTELLIGENCE

What is physical intelligence?

According to Howard Gardner in *Frames of Mind: The Theory of Multiple Intelligences* (1983), a person is capable of having a physical intelligence equal to his or her linguistic and numerical aptitudes. Physical intelligence is concerned with how we exercise control over our body and transform our immediate surroundings. It entails an inward management of the body's movements and an outward management of objects by the body. All animals and birds display the former—think of a running cheetah, a leaping dolphin, or a soaring eagle. The latter ability, however, is found in limited form only among certain primates: chimpanzees, for example, use sticks to reach termites and crack nuts against rocks. Human beings are the exception as they have continued to better themselves with the mental invention and the physical use of increasingly diverse and sophisticated tools across a range of tasks.

Manual dexterity

Physical intelligence includes the movement of select body parts such as the hands. Where the control of action and of external objects is involved, hands are of primary importance. Manual dexterity is divided into fine motor skills (the ability to regulate the pincer grip between finger and thumb and work with tiny objects), and gross motor skills (the ability to use the hand as a fist or grasp larger objects using the palm).

Coordination

The brain and the body are interacting constantly, with the brain directing the body's movements and the body feeding information back to the brain about its actions and position. Good coordination involves the two working well together and is the crux for successful movement.

Balance

The brain and the muscles work together to keep the body in equilibrium, or balanced, and protect it from any damage that could occur through falling. Occupations requiring good balance include scaffolders, gymnasts, and tree surgeons.

Reflexes

When the reaction speed to an event is more important than being accurate, this defence mechanism is known as a reflex. Grabbing a child about to fall, for example, evolved as a critical response to a dangerous situation.

Flexibility

In order to carry out physical activities using the widest possible range of movement you need flexibility. This mobility in your joints and muscles tends to lessen and become restricted with age, but regular stretching can alleviate this discomfort.

Why is physical intelligence important?

Recognizing control of our bodies and of physical movement in general as a type of intelligence may seem a little odd at first. Traditionally, mental and physical characteristics were viewed separately. Mental attributes, such as logical reasoning, were considered more special than physical attributes. Gardner's powerful counter-argument proposed that the brain was yet another body part to be directed and controlled. An intelligence factor is clearly present when carrying out physical movement. This is evident from the kinesthetic heights reached by world-class athletes as well as by the ability of actors and dancers in directly apprehending the actions, feelings, or dynamic movements of other people.

People who are physically intelligent are expert at controlling their bodies in creative movement like dancing and acting, crafts, and sports. They can mime other people's gestures or mimic mannerisms, relish taking objects apart and reassembling them, and tend to fidget when seated for long periods of time. Professional roles that require physical intelligence include builders, plumbers, illustrators, dancers, actors, sportspeople, mechanics, physical therapists, carpenters, chefs, surgeons, and jewelers.

Can you perform delicate tasks?

MANUAL DEXTERITY is the ability to control and use your hands. Fine motor tasks are those activities that involve precise and delicate movements of the fingers in a coordinated way. Keyhole surgery has pushed this skill to new levels, and it's vital to musicians of all kinds. Many leisure pastimes such as model-making, sewing, and painting also use fine motor movements.

If your brain and hands interact well together, you will be faster and more accurate at a range of everyday chores and jobs, both in the workplace and at home. Simple tasks, like putting on cufflinks, finding the right button in a box, leafing through a report, using a computer mouse, or even plucking your eyebrows, will all seem effortless.

Most people have a dominant hand, the one subconsciously chosen to undertake the majority of tasks. There are no standard criteria for measuring handedness, but the majority of people are right-handed (between 70-95%), the minority are left-handed (between 5-30%), and an unknown number are ambidexterous, equally skilled at using both hands.

The reasons for handedness are not known. There is evidence to show it is inherited, although the inclination to use one hand above the other can also be influenced and changed through practice.

TEST YOUR ABILITY

You will need a stopwatch or a clock with a second hand. Time your performance for speed and accuracy.

Transfer rice grains

Take 20 grains of rice, and two small bowls of equal size. Place one bowl either side of you. Pour the rice into one bowl and time how long it takes you to transfer each grain, one at a time, into the opposite bowl. Repeat with the other hand.

Tighten nuts and bolts

Take one narrow, two-inch bolt, and place 10 corresponding nuts next to you. Time how long it takes you to screw each nut down the neck of the bolt. Repeat with the other hand.

How different did each test feel using your favored hand? Was there a time difference between the two? Re-time yourself to practice your manual dexterity.

ANSWERS & INTERPRETATIONS

Over 25 seconds—you have average fine manual dexterity, a sound base for developing this ability even further. You probably found these tasks a bit fiddly, so find a hobby that allows you to practice coordinating your forefinger and thumb.

Under 25 seconds—you have excellent fine manual dexterity, and enjoy detailed and precise work, professionally or as a hobby. You use your forefinger and thumb in a very controlled manner to hold different instruments like a pen, knife, or needle.

Boosting tips

1. Play finger games when you're watching TV or sitting at your desk. Tap each finger once in sequence on the steering wheel or on your knee. Try each hand. Can you do this with both hands at the same time?

2. Practice doing everyday tasks with both your right and your left hand. Can you fasten buttons or lock your door with your non-preferred hand? Notice how different tasks feel using the hand you wouldn't normally favor and see whether, over time, the differences moderate.

Can you use your manual strength?

Manual dexterity also involves the ability to perform robust (gross) movements using your hands. Gross motor tasks such as using a hammer or throwing a ball, rely more on strength and employ the whole hand. While precision is not needed to the same degree as with fine motor tasks, people with good gross manual dexterity achieve incredible accuracy—like a golfer scoring a hole in one.

Gross motor skills are important for good development because they activate the large muscle movements used in running, jumping, climbing, and throwing. Children with good gross motor skills have strong posture and balance, and confidently control their bodies. Well-developed gross motor manual skills are important for a whole range of activities whether these be creative outlets like painting or modeling, scientific learning using construction materials, or musical tasks like playing drums or cymbals.

We use our hands on a daily basis to perform gross motor tasks: turning on faucets to run a bath, pulling on a shirt, pouring milk over breakfast cereal, driving, and so on. Many leisure activities like racquet sports, carpentry, baking, and gardening, are based on robust manual movements. Professions that make use of this ability include physical therapists, stage managers, and manufacturing engineers. Improving your gross manual dexterity will increase the fluidity and effectiveness of your hand movements.

TEST YOUR ABILITY

Catch the yo-yo

You will need a yo-yo.

Hold a fully wound yo-yo in your preferred hand. Slip your middle finger through the loop at the end of the string. Release the yo-yo from your palm, flicking your wrist to give the yo-yo momentum. Catch the yo-yo as it comes back up. Repeat 10 times.

Hit the ball

You will need a partner, a bat, and a ball.

Stand about 15 feet (4 m) apart. Your partner lobs the ball to you underhand. Hit the ball with the bat. Don't swing through with full force—just make contact with the ball. Repeat 10 times.

ANSWERS & INTERPRETATIONS

8 or less catches or hits—you have average gross manual dexterity, and probably enjoy using your hands in both delicate and robust tasks. Develop your ability to control your palm and fist through sports or hobbies such as baseball or tennis.

9 or more catches or hits—you have excellent gross manual dexterity, and probably excel at sports and do-it-yourself tasks. You can control your palm and fist very accurately, which enables you to manipulate larger objects like a ball, a drill, or a spade.

Boosting tips

1. Make a note of all the implements that you come to handle during the course of the day: keys, telephones, door handles, coins, pens, computer keyboards, and so on. Divide these objects into two categories—whether they mostly require gross or fine motor manual skills. Do you tend to favor one type of manual dexterity over the other?

2. Buy a stress ball and practice squeezing it under your desk, at home or at work. This will build up the muscles in your hands as well as relieve tension.

3. Handedness is even more marked with gross motor than with fine motor skills. Repeatedly experiment brushing your hair, cleaning your teeth, or dialing a phone with your non-dominant hand.

Do you have good hand-eye coordination?

HAND-EYE COORDINATION is the ability to use your eyes to guide hand movements. It develops in the first year of life, and continues to be refined and improved throughout adulthood. Writing, cutting, and sewing require precise hand-eye coordination, as do jobs in manufacturing and computer technology. Leisure activities such as stamp collecting, embroidery, and card playing, also use hand-eye coordination—working with our hands enables us to break away from the virtuality of modern technology.

A specialized manifestation of this type of coordination is sign language—a communication system of hand gestures that is interpreted visually. Although usually associated with the deaf community, 19th-century Native Americans, divided by different spoken dialects, used sign language to bridge the communication gap.

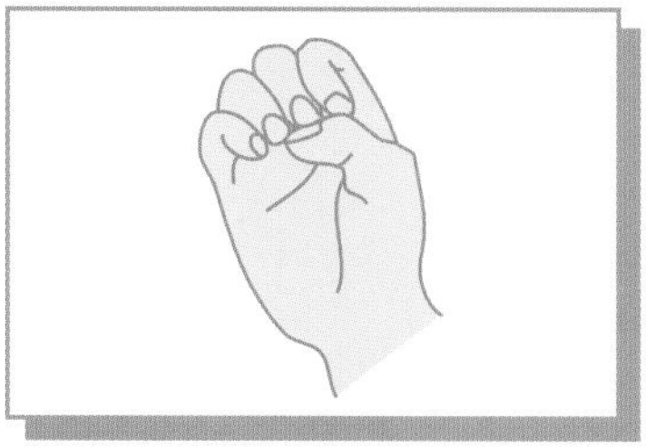

E

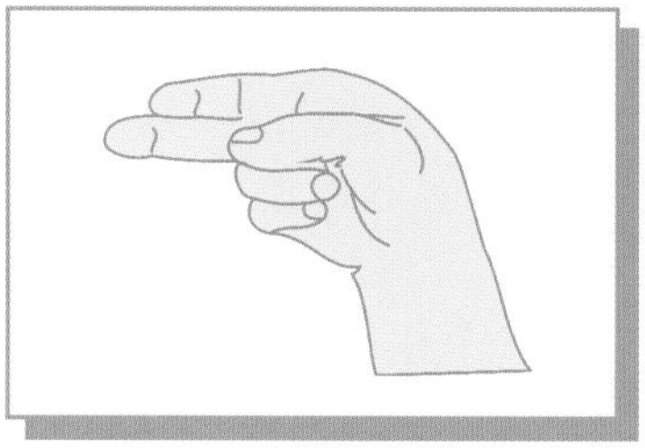

H

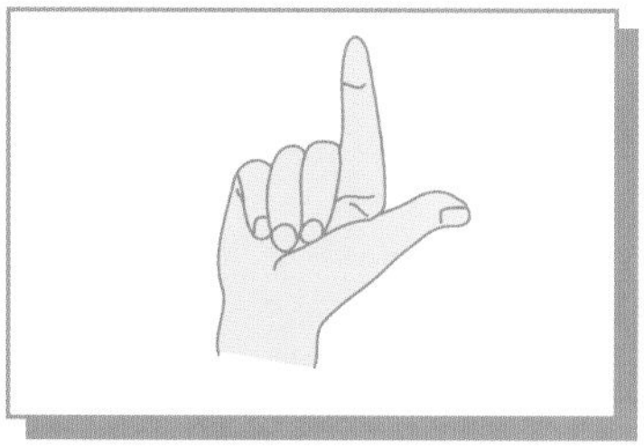

L

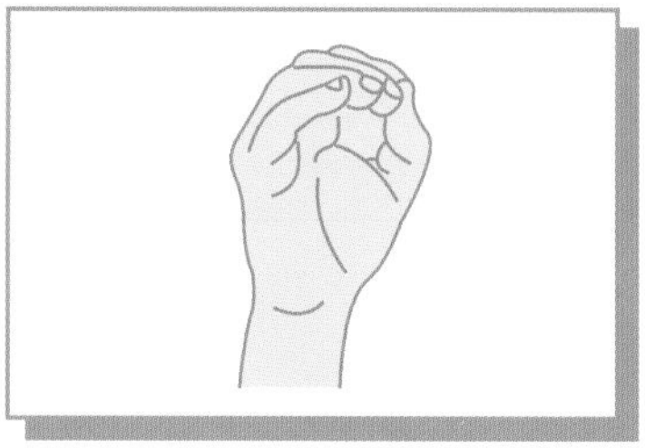

O

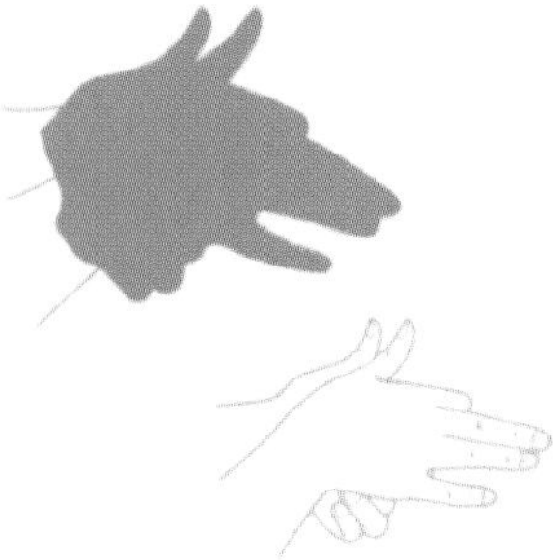

DOG

TURKEY

RABBIT

TEST YOUR ABILITY

Sign-spelling

Using the American Sign Language alphabet for the letters "h," "e," "l," and "o," spell out "hello" (*see opposite*). Practice this in front of the mirror until your movements are fluid.

Shadow puppetry

Practice these animal shapes in the dark by holding your hands in the positions illustrated (*see opposite*). Then shine a light on the wall behind your hands to reveal the shadow puppet.

ANSWERS & INTERPRETATIONS

If you were able to make most of the shapes, you have average hand-eye coordination, and may have found it hard to get your eyes, brain, and hands working in tune with one another. Develop hand-eye control by taking up an instrument or gardening.

If you were able to replicate all shapes with ease, you have excellent hand-eye coordination, and are able to duplicate a manual activity from your mind's eye. You are likely to perform any manual task skillfully and gracefully.

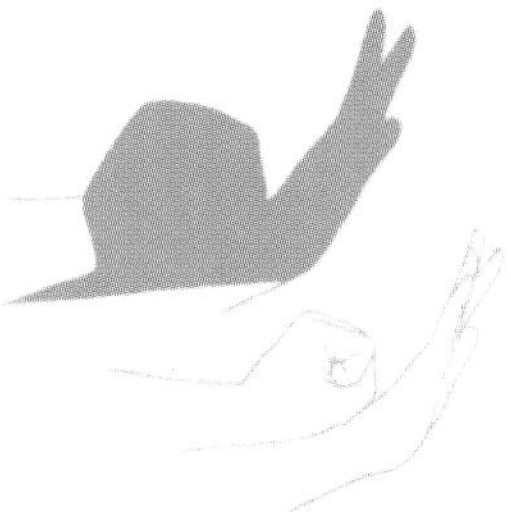

SNAIL

PANTHER

Boosting tips

1. Write down 20 six-digit "phone numbers." Practice dialing them quickly into a push button phone.

2. Play jacks using coins and paperclips. Spin a coin—you have until it falls flat to pick up as many paperclips as you can, one at a time.

3. If you can't touch-type, learning will transform the speed with which you access information from a computer screen or communicate in writing. Sit at the keyboard and type the following while looking at the screen rather than the keys: "The quick brown fox jumps over the lazy dog." Gradually increase your speed as you become more accurate.

Can you coordinate your body?

ALMOST ALL ANIMALS, from spiders to humans, have the capacity to produce coordinated motor performance. Survival depends on this ability.

The term coordination is used to describe two or more components functioning in harmony to achieve a desired movement pattern. Consider the action of walking. This can be viewed in terms of your arms and legs coordinating with each other as you move. On a more detailed level, individual muscle groups in your arms and legs are operating synergistically for smooth movement. At a micro level, the nervous system relays information from your brain to your arm and leg muscles. An understanding of one's own body and how it works in relation to itself, other objects, and people, is known as body coordination. It is partly a function of your brain's hard-wiring, but you can improve your raw ability through practice. People who have this talent are able to use their whole body to express feelings or ideas, and those who earn a living from doing this include athletes, circus performers, dancers, and actors.

TEST YOUR ABILITY

Cross your hands

Sit up on a chair with your feet squarely on the floor. Cross your hands so that your right hand rests on your left knee and your left hand on your right knee. Close your eyes. Keeping your hands crossed, bring your right foot up to touch your right hand. Repeat 10 times. Record the number of times you made a wrong, confused, or hesitant move.

Catch the ball

You will need a partner and a small ball.

Ask your partner to throw the ball either side of you, far away enough from you that you have to move your upper body to catch it. Repeat 10 times on your left or right side, in random order. Record the number of times you moved in the wrong direction or missed catching the ball.

ANSWERS & INTERPRETATIONS

If you made more than 2 errors—you have average body coordination. You may have felt clumsy and struggled to control your whole body in a single movement. Develop this skill while exercising or undertaking physical work.

If you made less than 2 errors—you have excellent body coordination,and probably enjoy sport because you are able to move your body gracefully in the way that you want and are less likely to expose yourself to physical injury.

Boosting tips

1. Write down 10 different body parts like "elbow," "chin," and "knee" on separate pieces of paper. Fold up each piece and put it into one pile. Write down "left" and "right" alternatively 5 times each. Fold up each piece and place them into a second pile. Pick out four pieces of paper at random, two from each pile. Touch those "combination" body parts that come up: for example, with "right," "knee," "left," and "shoulder," your right knee needs to touch your left shoulder. Some combinations may not be possible!

2. Try juggling with three balls or oranges. See how long you can keep items up in the air without dropping any of them.

3. Take a walk, and avoid stepping on the cracks in the sidewalk. Walk gracefully so that no one knows what you are actually doing.

Can you balance objects?

BALANCE CAN be defined as the body's ability to maintain a posture. This involves coordinating the body's center of gravity with whichever part is in contact with the ground as you kneel, sit, or even stand on your head. Your center of gravity will change with each position.

Remaining steady is harder if you're balancing a moving load, yet the brain automatically adjusts to these changes as we walk, jump, or run. When we hold or position an object, the brain has to re-tune information about muscle tension and movement quickly and accurately. If you are carrying a heavy box, your brain will instantly recognize that your body is struggling to keep balanced as you move. This can be exhausting and is a well-known source of muscular injury.

Learning to shift your body's center of gravity deliberately is a good exercise for improving your sense of balance. Although your body will always have to make adjustments as you move, some exercise techniques, such as Pilates, aim to minimize and control these changes through specific gravity-shifting movements.

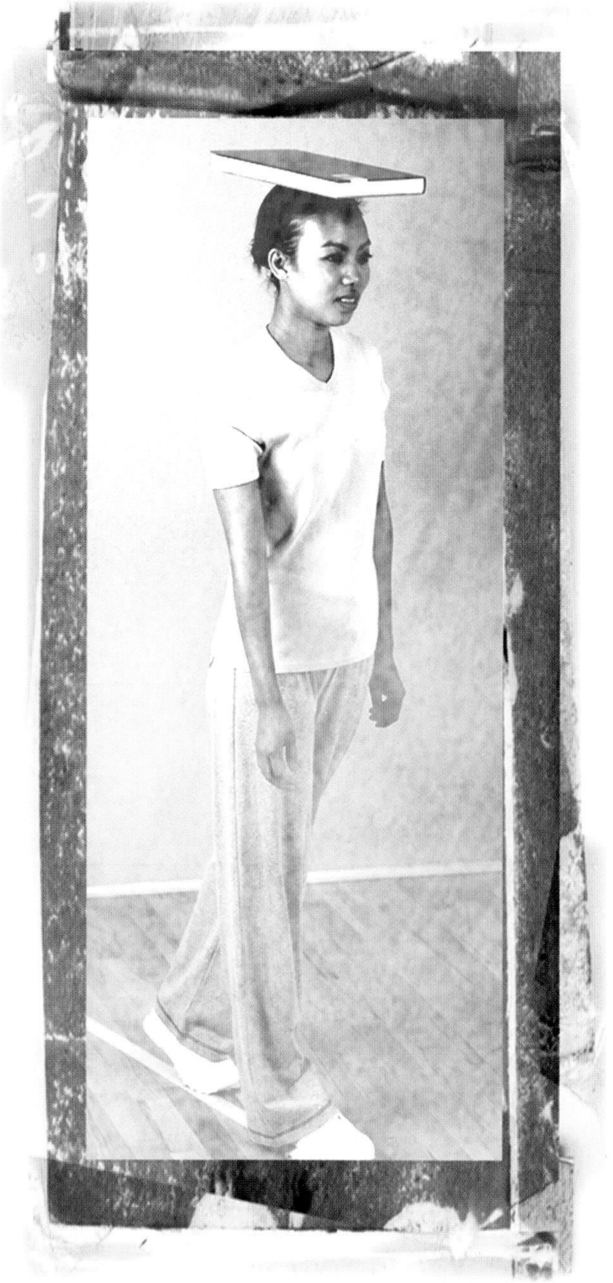

TEST YOUR ABILITY

Bounce a ball

You will need a large, bouncy ball like a soccer ball.

Standing in place, bounce the ball with one knee 10 consecutive times without using your hands to catch or steady it. Note how many times you needed to use your hand to keep the ball steady.

Balance a book

You will need masking tape, a hard floor, and a hardback book.

On the floor, mark out a straight line with the tape. Stand where it begins and balance the book on your head. Take 5 steps, turn on your heel, take another 5 steps. Come back. Note the times you used your hand to steady the book.

ANSWERS & INTERPRETATIONS

If you used your hands at all, you have average object balance, and probably find it difficult to control objects that you are unable to firmly hold for whatever reason. Developing overall body balance will enhance this skill.

If you didn't use your hands at all, you have excellent object balance and control objects skillfully and carefully. You probably find it easy to balance garden tools on your shoulder, or a pile of folders in your arms.

Boosting tips

1. Using the line you marked out for the balancing test, take 10 heel-to-toe steps, turn on the balls of your feet and take 10 steps back. Practice until you are able to complete the exercise without wobbling. Also try this on tiptoe or by hopping on one leg.

2. Challenge your sense of balance by removing some of the clues your brain receives from other body parts. Balance a stem glass in the palm of your hand with your eyes closed, or keep a magazine level on your head while your arms are tucked behind your back.

Can you balance your body?

ADJUSTING YOUR center of gravity to match your movements is known as body balance. It enables you to undertake and sustain a position or an activity. This is relevant when in contact with the ground or using a substitute—riding a bike, walking on a plank, jumping on a trampoline, or skipping.

Building any type of structure requires solid foundations that will withstand changes in physical conditions. As your fitness foundation, balance is no exception and can be categorized into static balance (maintaining a position) and dynamic balance (remaining stable while moving). Even slight changes in surface terrain will require constant and considerable muscular adjustments within the joints: think of the classic twisted ankle scenario. A deterioration or a weakness in balance can increase the risk of sprains and strains in both amateur and professional athletes. Improving poor balance will keep brain and body in tune with one another and prevent unnecessary injury.

The "control tower" of the body's ability to balance itself lies in the inner ear within three, tiny, fluid-filled tubes. Any movement of this fluid feeds balance information to the brain, and each tube is set at a different angle to the others, so together they monitor gravity, acceleration, head movement and position. Balance disorders like vertigo, are caused when the inner ear wrongly tells your brain that your head is spinning.

TEST YOUR ABILITY

Dynamic balance

You will need to find a straight and flat length of curb.

Stand on your left leg on the edge of the curb. Take 10 hops forward. Turn around. Take 10 steps back on your right leg. Count the times you lose your balance or your feet touch the gutter. Alternately use a plank of wood about 6 feet (1.8 m) long, 1 foot (30 cm) off the ground at one end, and 6 inches (15 cm) at the other.

Static balance

You will need 2 tennis balls.

Place a tennis ball under each foot and balance yourself, ensuring that neither your toe or heel are actually touching the floor. Maintain this position for 20 seconds. Count the number of times that any part of your foot makes contact with the floor.

ANSWERS & INTERPRETATIONS

If your foot touched the floor 2 times or more—you have average body balance, and may have struggled to maintain a pose without flailing your arms about. Practicing balance poses will force your body to center itself rather than relying on your arms.

If your foot touched the floor 2 times or less—you have excellent body balance, and can move around confidently and accurately. You probably do not have to use your arms as much to balance because your body is centered and strong.

Boosting tips

1. Go to the park and try marching for a few minutes on both even and uneven surfaces. Try standing or hopping on one leg. Compare your performance across tasks. Practice until you reach a similar level of competency on both surfaces.

2. Attempt walking with just one shoe on. You may feel clumsy at first, but your body will soon adjust.

Do you respond quickly?

A RAPID MOVEMENT to a given stimulus causes a response or a reaction time known as a reflex. Reflex movements may involve the whole body such as running away from danger, or specific body parts such as pulling back your hand when it touches something hot. Reflexes developed as an evolutionary method of escape from situations of immediate danger such as attacks by wild animals. Nowadays we are shielded from most physical dangers, but driving and riding in a car, a truck, or on a motorcycle still present a commonplace and daily danger. If we were about to hit or be hit by an incoming vehicle, for example, we would use our reflexes to escape the collision or minimize the consequences.

One area that has been well documented in the search for greater car safety is drivers' reaction times. There are several categories and examples including simple reaction time (the time it takes you to brake if a child runs out into the road, for example); discrimination reaction time (the time it takes you to react if a child runs out into the road against the time it takes you to react if a piece of paper accidentally falls on the road); and choice reaction time (the time it takes you to decide to brake depending on whether it is a child that runs, or a ball that rolls on to the road). When a driver stops his or her car suddenly, over half the braking distance is due to the driver response time, rather than the mechanics of the car. Increase your reflex response time and become both a safer driver and pedestrian.

TEST YOUR ABILITY

Catching reflex
You will need a 12-inch (30-cm) ruler and a partner.

Your partner holds the ruler vertically (number 12 at the top.) Place your forefinger and thumb either side of the bottom of the ruler without touching it. Your partner lets go of it without warning and you need to catch it as quickly as you can. Record the average inches that fell before you caught the ruler. Repeat 3 times.

Throwing reflex
You will need a partner and a large ball.

Stand about 15 feet (4 m) away, but facing your partner. Ask him or her to throw you the ball. Clap your hands before catching the ball. Repeat 10 times.

ANSWERS & INTERPRETATIONS

If the ruler dropped by 6 inches (15 cm) or more, or you missed the ball—you have average reflex responses, and probably found it difficult to react quickly enough. If your concentration improves, your responses will quicken.

If the ruler dropped by 6 inches (15 cm) or less, or you caught every throw—you have excellent reflex responses, which are vital to have in safety situations. You probably also excel at racket sports like tennis or baseball.

Boosting tips

1. Type "reaction time" into any Internet browser for a host of relevant sites where you can test your reflex online by clicking on the mouse to a stimulus such as the screen changing color. Your response time is monitored and recorded.

2. Write down a list of situations that you feel would benefit from an increase in your reaction time, like answering a ringing phone or catching a falling object before it breaks. Choose one task and practice doing it.

Can you challenge your reflexes?

Reflexes, reaction times, and speed responses involve mental, physical, innate, and learned factors. The brain processes a sensation or a stimulus and then selects a response. Movement is initiated when muscles perform the necessary actions. We are all born with inherent neuromuscular capabilities. Although individual differences do exist, everyone can learn to improve his or her reaction time.

Age affects reaction time. From childhood until your late 20s, reflex response times get better, then slowly worsen in your 50s and 60s, rapidly declining from your 70s onward. Research has shown that men are faster than women, and that this difference between the sexes doesn't decrease with practice. Your reaction time will be considerably better if you are given warning that a reaction is imminently required of you. Likewise you will tend to slow down if you make a mistake, so as not to repeat it. Fitness is also a key issue.

The advantages of having fast reflexes are twofold: to protect either yourself or others and to improve overall sporting performance. Examples of the former include putting out a fire in the kitchen, catching a toddler before he or she falls, or moving quickly and nimbly enough to dodge a falling object before it hits you.

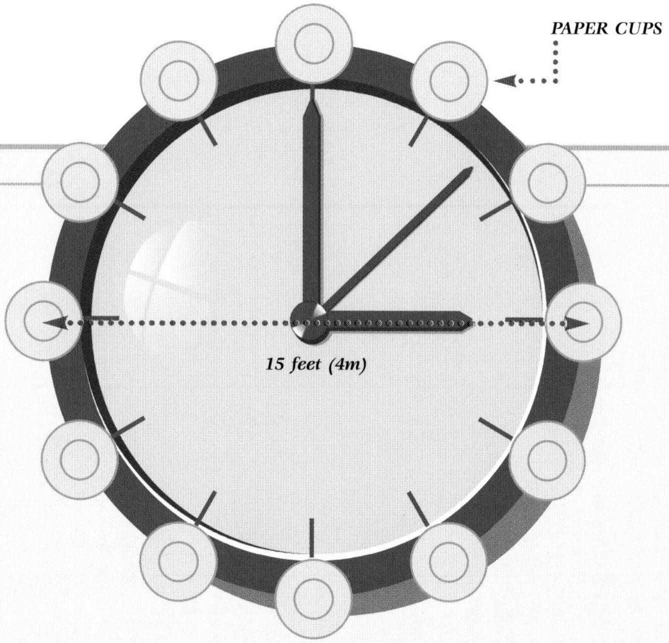

TEST YOUR REFLEXES

Running clock

You will need a partner, a stopwatch or a clock with a second hand, and 12 paper cups or floor markers. Time the speed and accuracy of your performance.

Using the cups, mark out the numbers on a "clockface" 15 feet (4 m) in diameter. Stand in its center—ask your partner to start the stopwatch and call out a random number from one to 12. As soon as you hear the number, run

Boosting tips

1. Throw a small object like a ball or a pen to and fro between each hand, catching it each time.

2. Time yourself in everyday situations: how long it takes you to reach the street outside your office block from your desk; from your bathroom to your bedroom; from the entrance of the subway to the platform. The added pressure of wanting to better your last time will help develop your reflex ability.

ANSWERS & INTERPRETATIONS

If you completed both tasks in more than 45 seconds—you have average reflexes, and may have difficulty bringing your whole body into action quickly and accurately. Develop your reflexes by preparing your body for action—much of the reflex response is physiological.

If you completed both tasks in less than 45 seconds—you have excellent reflexes and the gift of being able to coordinate your entire body to react quickly. This is essential in timed sports like athletics or motor racing, and will be a vital element in securing your safety if you find yourself having to flee from a dangerous situation.

to it, then return to your starting position. Your partner should call out a second number immediately on your return to the center of the clock. Repeat until all numbers from one to 12 have been called out. Record your total time.

Bouncing ball

You will need a partner, a stopwatch or a clock with a second hand, two different-sized bouncy balls, and some masking tape.

Tape the two balls together so that they are securely fastened. Stand about 15 feet (4 m) away from your partner, and ask him or her to bounce the balls on the ground toward you. The bouncing height and direction of each ball will be erratic. Retrieve the ball and throw it back to your partner. Repeat 10 times, timing yourself on your speed and accuracy.

Are you limber?

FLEXIBILITY, MOBILITY, and suppleness are all terms used to describe the degree of limb movement around joints. Performing a joint action through a range of movement involves two types of muscles—protagonistic (to cause movement) and antagonistic (to oppose movement). These two groups determine the amount of mobility possible.

As they age, muscles lose elasticity, so regular stretching is crucial to maintain flexibility, increase wellbeing and prevent injury during everyday activity. For those who enjoy sport, it can make the difference between winning and losing, and pre- and post-workout stretching is recommended to clients by all fitness trainers. Muscles support your skeleton and also protect your joints. Their intervention maintains the necessary balance between protection and movement. If joints become hypermobile (overstretched), they can run the risk of injury. Conversely, if joints are hypomobile (understretched), joint movement is restricted and can even be painful. Good flexibility and regular stretching will help you to move efficiently and safely throughout your life.

Both Pilates and yoga are excellent for increasing flexibility through stretching and relaxation. Many people with stressful lives endorse the therapeutic properties of these exercise disciplines.

TEST YOUR FLEXIBILITY

Leg raises

Step 1

Step 1 Lie on your back. Raise your right leg as high as you can and lift your left leg slightly off the ground. Bring your chin to your chest and try to reach for your ankles or toes.
Step 2 Switch your legs in a "scissor action" without lowering your arms.

Step 2

Boosting tips

1. Make time to stretch at your desk at work or while watching TV at home. Stretch your neck, shoulders, chest, arms, back, hips, and legs. Work out a routine and sequence in which you attempt the stretch, relax into it, then push yourself a bit further. It may feel a little uncomfortable at first, but do stop if you feel any pain.

2. Practice deep breathing. Inhale deeply until your lungs are full of air. Hold for 5 seconds. Exhale slowly. Repeat until you feel completely relaxed.

ANSWERS & INTERPRETATIONS

If you were able to do these stretches, but require further practice to complete them with ease—you have average flexibility, and may simply not have been relaxed enough to achieve the stretches. An essential component of flexibility is the ability to relax.

If you were able to complete these stretches to hold your ankles or toes—you have excellent flexibility, and each time were able to relax fully into the stretches. Pushing yourself a little further each time can help improve your flexibility.

The "v" stretch

Step 1 Sit with your arms out at shoulder height, legs open in front of you.
Step 2 Reach your hand down toward the little toe of the opposite foot.
Step 3 Repeat on the other side, keeping your head in a neutral position.

Can you improve your flexibility?

THE FLUID MOVEMENTS of muscles and joints are essential to both physical and mental disciplines. Joseph Pilates (1881–1967), a German physiologist, developed a variety of controlled exercises, designed to be repeated and performed in sequence as an aid to promoting the recovery of injured dancers. One of the major benefits of Pilates is increased suppleness, particularly important after a sedentary day at your desk or driving in your car.

Yoga, the mind-body practice, attempts to unite body and mind through a series of physical poses and breathing techniques. There are many forms of yoga, but its key elements always involve a sequence of poses coupled with breathing and relaxation techniques, all of which use stretching movements to achieve flexibility.

TEST YOUR FLEXIBILITY

Pilates pose

Step 1 Stretch your legs out in front of you. Open them slightly wider than hip width. Flex your feet. Stretch and lift your arms to shoulder height. Engage your buttocks and lift yourself up and out of your hips as you breathe. Sit up with your back straight.

Step 2 Tuck your chin into your chest and firmly pull your navel toward your spine as you reach forward with your arms. Your body should form a "c" curve from the top of your head down to your tailbone. Breathe out. Come back up until you are sitting upright.

Boosting tips

1. Make sure that your sitting positions at home and at work are not cramping your muscles by making you hunch over your desk or slump on the sofa. Remember to keep your back straight and your body "open" to prevent unnecessary tensing up. A relaxed body position helps maintain flexibility.

2. Incorporate a full body stretch into your waking up routine. Lie on the bed, for example, raise your arms above your head, and point your feet. Imagine you are being pulled by your fingers and your toes. Hold for 5 seconds. Relax.

ANSWERS & INTERPRETATIONS

If you were able to do these stretches, but require further practice to complete them with ease—you have average flexibility. The more flexible you become, the less you put yourself at risk of suffering injuries like strains.

If you were able to extend these stretches to hold your ankle or toes—you have excellent flexibility. You either stretch regularly as part of your routine or are blessed with supple joints. Flexibility is crucial in protecting your body from sprains.

Yoga pose

Step 1 Stand with your feet about 3 feet (1 m) apart. They should be facing forward. Keep your arms at shoulder level.

Step 2 Turn your right foot out by 90° and your left foot in by about 30°. Place your right hand on your right thigh. Extend your left arm up. Inhale and stretch through your left hand.

Step 3 Exhale and slide your right hand down your thigh. Slowly bend to the side, feeling the stretch through the left half of your body. Turn your head up toward the ceiling.

Step 4 Stretch through your left arm. Slide far down your leg, grasping your ankle if you can.

Your physical intelligence

NOW THAT YOU'VE completed all the tests, you can profile your results to get an overall view of your strengths. Check the relevant boxes for each of your test scores.

Did you discover your body to be just a tool, or a means of expressing who you are?

- If you have 7 or more checks in the average column, you have adequate physical intelligence. You are likely to use your body as a means for everyday living doing simple physical tasks like sitting, standing, answering the phone, and using a keyboard.

	Average ✓	*Excellent* ✓
MANUAL DEXTERITY		
Test 1 (pages 136-37)		
Test 2 (pages 138-39)		
COORDINATION		
Test 1 (pages 140-41)		
Test 2 (pages 142-43)		
BALANCE		
Test 1 (pages 144-45)		
Test 2 (pages 146-47)		
REFLEX		
Test 1 (pages 148-49)		
Test 2 (pages 150-51)		
FLEXIBILITY		
Test 1 (pages 152-53)		
Test 2 (pages 154-55)		

- If you have 3-4 checks in either column, you have good physical intelligence. You are likely to have a fairly active lifestyle, but are not a sport all-rounder.
- If you have 7 or more checks in the excellent column, you have superior physical intelligence. You are likely to enjoy sport activities and have a high level of fitness.

Developing and improving physical intelligence

Physical intelligence can be measured using conceptually concrete units like time, weight, and distance. Your kinesthetic profile may have surprised you or simply confirmed what you already suspected about your general physical aptitude.

As one of the abilities most susceptible to improvement, physical excellence (and intelligence) can be attained through sheer determination. It is important from the outset, however, to consider whether you want to develop control of your body's movements, or are looking to increase its control over objects (using hands or tools).

If you possess adequate-to-good physical intelligence, remember that traditional sport represents only one way of improving regulation of your body's movements. Dancing and acting are highly rewarding whole body experiences which require the integration of other skills including social, spatial, and musical abilities. Arts and crafts activities, such as sculpture, collage, interior decorating, or model-making, develop object control skills.

If you have superior physical intelligence, it can be easy to focus on a particular sport or activity you are good at, but try to stretch yourself by applying your physical intelligence to all parts of your body. If you enjoy playing golf, try a contact sport that involves more aerobic exercise. If you play a lot of different sports, concentrate on building up your skill and fitness in one or two activities.

Working with children

If you have or look after youngsters, it can be fascinating to witness their physical development in the making: physical self-control is gradually expressed by the sitting-standing-walking-running developmental sequence. The control of objects starts in early infancy, with babies being able to manipulate objects. Toddlers can handle tools, even if clumsily, and older children rapidly progress to using and making their own implements in increasingly sophisticated ways. It would seem that children are genetically programmed to develop physical abilities on their own, but they require encouragement and support. You could, for example, provide this input by:

- Choosing nursery rhymes and songs together which involve acting out a range of actions like "Row, Row, Row Your Boat" for the upper body, or "Ring o' Roses" for lower body actions.
- Helping older children write and perform a play, cabaret, or revue. Include traditional acting, singing, miming, and dancing.
- Encouraging children to be active. Ride bikes together, go skating, take youngsters to the park or the local swimming pool, and play ball games.

7

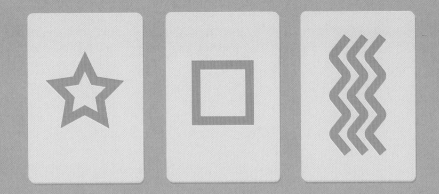

OTHER TYPES OF

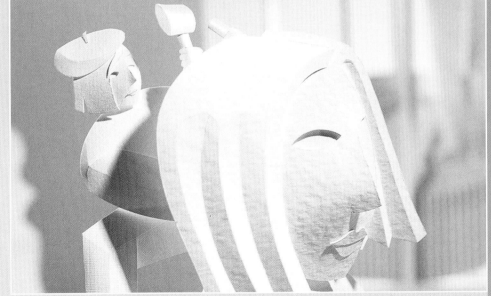

INTELLIGENCE

What are creative, musical, naturalistic, and intuitive intelligence?

THE IMPACT OF multiple intelligence has led psychologists to examine other possible areas of specialized ability, four of which are addressed in this chapter. Naturalistic and musical intelligence are recognized by multiple intelligence researchers, and studies into creative and musical intelligence have extended the debate on multiple intelligence theory.

Creative intelligence

Logical intelligence, the ability to digest information systematically, draws on the type of thinking called "convergent"—its aim is to arrive at a single answer to a problem. The purpose of the converse form of thinking, known as "divergent," is to generate new ideas and information to produce several solutions.

Creative thinking relies on different thinking styles and abilities such as:

- Originality, which allows you come up with unusual ideas and truly think outside of the box. You do not feel confined by standard ways of doing things and challenge the norm;
- Flexibility, which generates ideas from as many different categories as possible to cross over the usual boundaries. Not all great ideas are particularly original: air conditioning, for example, was used in homes before someone applied it to cars (now an industry standard);

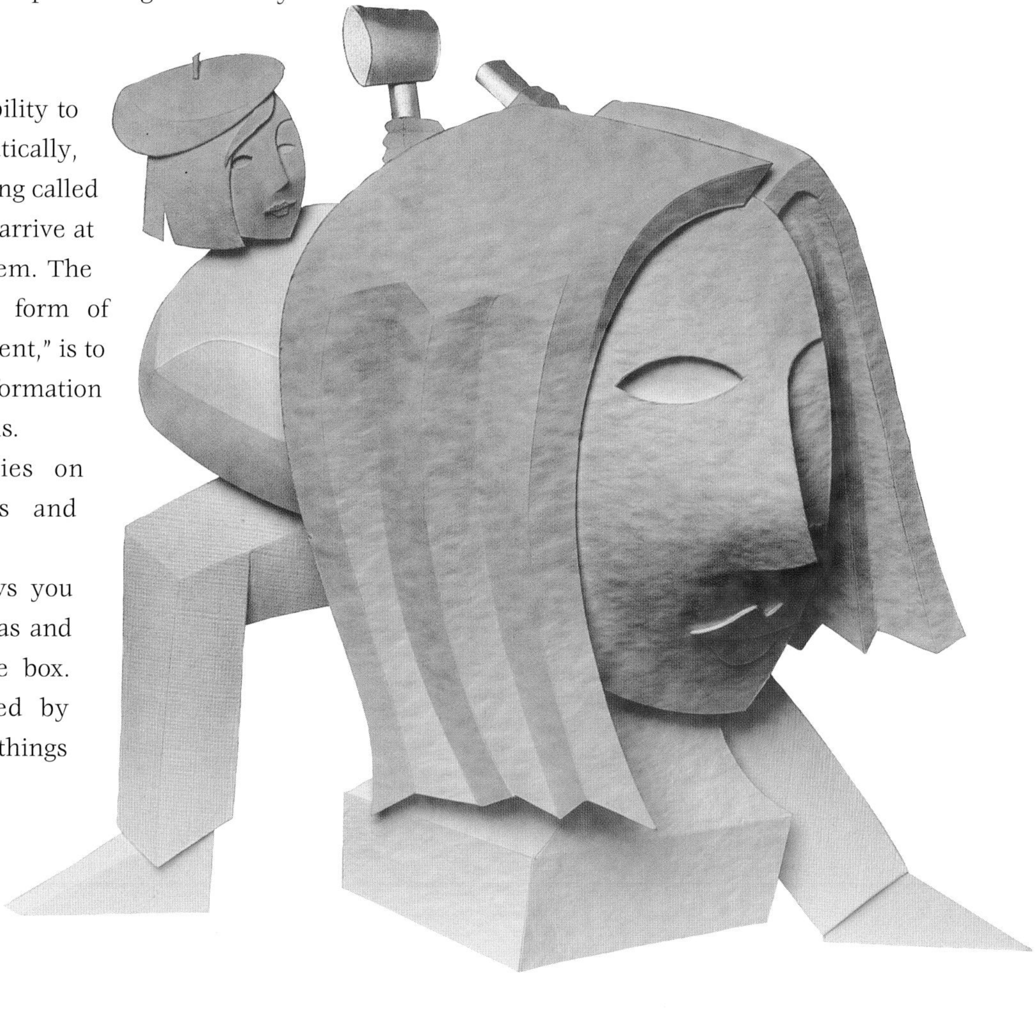

- Fluency, which enables you to generate many ideas to form the base of a decision-making "pyramid";
- Elaboration, which permits ideas to dynamically feed off each other, and be extended or embellished.

Musical intelligence

The ability to perceive, create, and express music in all its forms is known as musical intelligence. This skill can be "top-down"—an empathic and intuitive appreciation of music. An example of this is someone uplifted and inspired by musical notes and beats. It can also be "bottom-up"—an analytical and technical understanding of music. Someone who composes and performs music possesses bottom-up musical skill.

Music can be broken down into two core constituents: pitch (musical notes or melody) and rhythm (the beat or the timing of the notes). Pitch is the highness or lowness of a musical sound as determined by the speed of the vibrations producing it. Musical rhythm is about time structure such as the patterns of lengths in a group of notes. A third musical element is timbre (the quality and "color" of a particular tone).

Musical intelligence develops early (evident from musical protégés), a parent's lullaby soothes even tiny babies, and toddlers can produce single tones and copy parts of familiar songs. The Suzuki Talent Education Program in Japan trains pre-schoolers to reach extraordinary heights in playing string instruments. Interestingly though, early musical promise does not always last into adulthood.

Naturalistic intelligence

The ability to nurture, identify and classify plants, animals, and natural phenomena is known as naturalistic intelligence. It recognizes the intelligence of people who can track down animals, navigate by the stars, or grow their own crops. People with this intelligence probably loved being outdoors as children, enjoyed keeping pets, growing plants from seed, collecting fossils, or observing the weather. They are keenly aware of any changes in their environment through their senses.

Intuitive intelligence

The ability to decipher patterns from seemingly chaotic information takes place deep in our subconscious and is known as intuitive intelligence. Have you ever had a solution to a problem suddenly pop into your head? Your brain stores everything that occurs around you, sorts through it, and "files" away this information for future use. When a new revelation leaps into your mind, it is your intuition at work!

Commonly thought of in terms of "gut feelings" or ethereal experiences like extrasensory perception, the importance of intuition is now taking root even in the normally sceptical, hard-edged corporate world. Entrepreneurs often succeed because they "listen" to their intuition—they often admit to just having had a feeling about a certain business idea whereas, in practice, the brain was patiently and subconsciously logging in and processing events and ideas until a business proposition took conscious form.

Why are creative, musical, naturalistic, and intuitive intelligence important?

Multiple intelligence theory is broader than the established categories of logical, spatial, linguistic, emotional, and physical intelligence. This overarching, all-inclusive philosophical concept on intelligence has led other psychologists to embrace further facets including the more elusive creative and intuitive intelligences.

Creative intelligence

Convergent (non-creative) and divergent (creative) thinking are used in all aspects of life. The latter is useful when successfully dealing with change in a fast-paced world. However, we spend much of our educational careers logically and methodically working through masses of information, tasks, and syllabuses based on the assumption that there are right and wrong answers, so convergent thinking is ingrained from an early age. Once we embark on our professional careers, the joint ability to be both creative about problems and able to fuse available information in different ways, is highly valued.

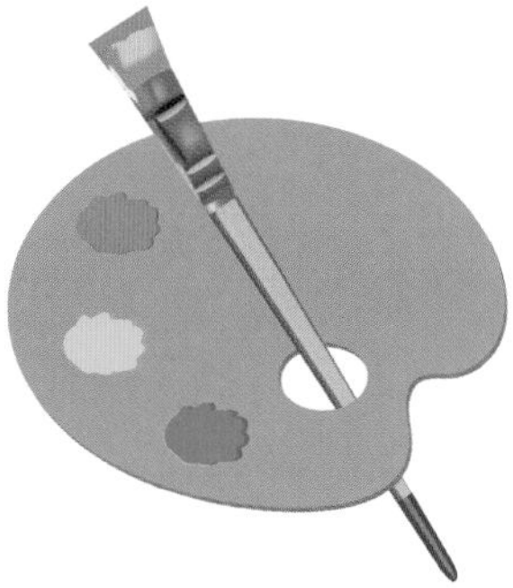

Creatively intelligent people excel at thinking in a spontaneous, free-flowing way. Not phased by wacky or unusual ideas, they are skilled at postponing judgment, and at compartmentalizing thought processes to ensure ideas flourish and are not killed off by practical considerations. These people make good designers, artists, researchers, product developers, and media professionals.

Musical intelligence

Music is ever-present in our lives: at home, in the car, while shopping, in restaurants, at religious services, even at school. It helps us to learn and remember: if you hear an old song on the radio, the likelihood is that you'll recall the words as memories are evoked. Music has the power to soothe, inspire, energize, and transport.

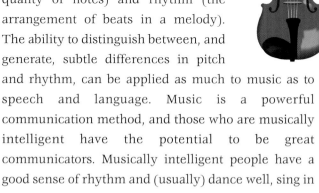

Music possesses two core components: pitch (the auditory quality of notes) and rhythm (the arrangement of beats in a melody). The ability to distinguish between, and generate, subtle differences in pitch and rhythm, can be applied as much to music as to speech and language. Music is a powerful communication method, and those who are musically intelligent have the potential to be great communicators. Musically intelligent people have a good sense of rhythm and (usually) dance well, sing in tune, detect when a note is off-key, remember and recognize songs, mimic accents, do impressions of people, and mentally compose songs or melodies. They make excellent musicians, performers, composers, interpreters, impresarios, music critics, and sound engineers.

Naturalistic intelligence

At first glance, living in the city would largely seem to preclude the need for understanding and being able to interpret the natural world. In fact, there are practical considerations: we still need people to grow food for us, predict the weather, and keep insect pests under control. There are also emotional benefits to be reaped from getting more in touch with your naturalistic side. People feel better when they get some fresh air, care for a pet, look after house plants, or tend a small garden. They feel calmer, less stressed, more able to cope with the demands of modern city life. Naturalistically intelligent people have great empathy with other living beings, and can successfully nurture and classify them. They are familiar with their environment and how nature interacts with it, and represent the natural choice for biologists, ecologists, astronomers, wildlife photographers, chemists, and landscape gardeners.

Intuitive intelligence

Humans are skilled at managing information, sifting through facts and impressions to focus on important details, then processing them to arrive at a final conclusion. Sometimes information is so widely scattered from its source that it's almost impossible to detect a connection. When logical and conscious thought let us down, we can't group relevant data, so information remains compartmentalized or fails to register. Intuition is our subconscious "safety net," an insightful, deep-seated way of collecting the information that our conscious mind might have discarded or may have missed. Intuitively intelligent people see the bigger picture to come up with ideas, concepts, and relationships that others often overlook, and recognize that the subconscious brain is as important as its conscious counterpart. They make great psychologists, entrepreneurs, teachers, journalists, and religious leaders.

Are you a lateral thinker?

ROTATING A PROBLEM from different angles to try and locate alternative points of entry involves lateral thinking. This is the sort of creative processing that the human mind can do, but computers are unable to. It is useful when one train of thought reaches a dead end and another approach is needed. In many real-life situations, logical thinking can be restricting and may inhibit a full exploration of the issues at hand, so thinking laterally helps us to reach a solution. Lateral thinking puzzles are bizarre situations that require an explanation. They can be very difficult but satisfying to solve and will encourage you to examine your expectations or prejudices about a given situation from piecing together lots of different clues and bits of information. Thinking laterally and avoiding the obvious is a great tool in life that, once developed, you will turn to frequently, whether in choosing an unusual gift for a friend, writing an original presentation to customers, or designing the décor of your new apartment.

TEST YOUR LATERAL THINKING

Work out what is going on in the offbeat situations below. Take your time and be open-minded, flexible, and creative in your thinking approach.

1. A man sat in his car at night while rain poured on his windshield. Suddenly, the street lights went out and the rain stopped. Where was he?

2. A scarf, a carrot, two lumps of coal, and three buttons were discovered in a garden. How did they get there?

3. A man lies alone and dead in a field, wearing a knapsack. How did he die?

4. A man watched his wife jump from a bridge and then celebrated this over a meal. Why?

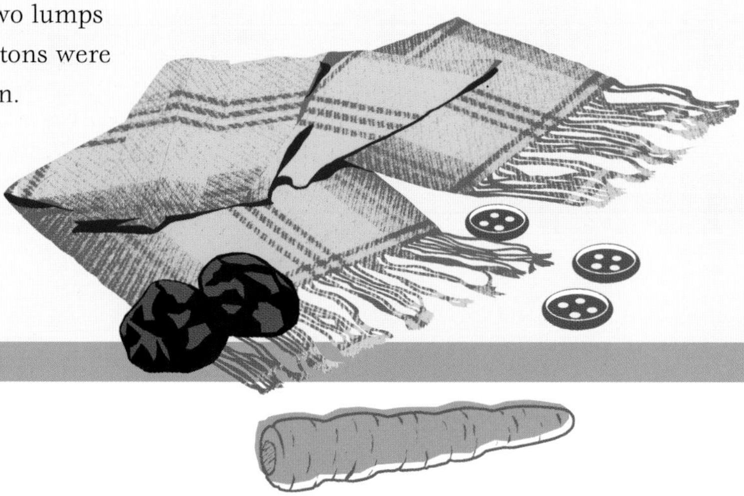

Boosting tip

Write a list of all the things you do out of habit—like get a cappuccino from the same coffee shop on your way to work every morning. Next to each one, identify as many alternatives to these habits as you can think of—buy a fruit smoothie instead, try another coffee shop, take a different route into work. Generate five different options for each habit. Pick one option from each to put into action.

5. A horse jumps over a castle and is captured by a bishop. Where did this happen?

6. A woman has two daughters who were born at the same hour of the same day of the same year, but they weren't twins. How can this be?

7. A father and son were injured in a car crash and were rushed to hospital. On seeing the boy on the operating table, the surgeon exclaimed, "That's my son!" How can this be?

8. Bonnie and Clyde are lying dead on the floor. They are surrounded by glass shards from a broken bowl. There are no marks on their bodies and they weren't poisoned. How did they die?

ANSWERS & INTERPRETATIONS

Score 1 point for each correct answer
Maximum score = 8

1. In a carwash during a power failure.
2. They belonged to a snowman that had melted.
3. His parachute failed to open.
4. She had just completed a bungee jump.
5. On a chessboard.
6. They were two from a set of triplets.
7. The surgeon was the boy's mother.
8. Bonnie and Clyde are goldfish whose bowl was knocked over and smashed on the floor.

If you scored 2 points or less—you have average lateral thinking and probably thought the answers were way out and slightly ridiculous. Your tendency is for deductive rather than lateral thinking. Past experience is often used as a point of reference when making decisions, but it could limit you because the best solution may be something that you've never done before. Try to question the importance of previous events in taking future decisions.

If you scored 3 points or more—you have excellent lateral thinking and probably enjoy thinking outside of the box and are valued for your creative contributions to problem-solving. You are not rule-bound or afraid to break the mold.

Can you brainstorm ideas?

There are a number of powerful creative thinking techniques that unlock and promote creative thinking processes. Thinking without some sort of structure is sometimes difficult, but nearly everyone is able to exercise some degree of creativity—it simply needs to be unblocked.

Brainstorming, which involves producing ideas in a creative and unstructured environment, is the most well-known idea-generating method. A single idea is used to generate other ideas. Everything is recorded, nothing is disregarded or criticized. It helps break down habit-bound thinking to produce a set of ideas which can then be reviewed simply on their value or merit. This technique is useful for challenging problems, where fresh choices, rather than obvious and hackneyed ones, are required.

The key quality of brainstorming is the quantity of ideas that need to be generated. A large amount is all-important as the usual, stale ideas tend to come to mind first, so the first 20-30 ideas are probably not going to be the most innovative and creative ones. Also, the larger the list of possibilities, the more material there is to choose from, adapt, or act upon as inspiration for more concepts. Why limit yourself to one solution when working on a problem?

TEST YOUR ABILITY

You can do this brainstorming session alone or in a small group (ideally around 4-6 people). There are four cardinal rules: firstly, set aside about 20 minutes; secondly, suspend all judgment until the time is up; thirdly, write down all ideas so everyone who participates can see them and try to build on the ideas of others; fourthly, come up with as many ideas as you can.

Test 1

For 20 minutes, brainstorm 30 ideas on the uses of a rope (for example, belt, dog leash, lasso). Distill these into three practical and innovative ideas for new or creative ways of using a rope.

Test 2

For 20 minutes, brainstorm 30 ideas for improving car design (for example, a gas tank that fills itself, non-puncture tires, built-in fridge). Distill these into three practical and effective ideas.

Boosting tip

Approaching a problem from different angles is vital for creative thinking. Imagine a bunch of keys in terms of: what you see (uniform metal objects with a jagged edge), feel (cool and hard surfaces), hear (jangling sound), smell (nothing much), and taste (metallic). Now think about a bunch of keys in terms of: who? what? where? when? how? why? Who do these keys belong to? What are they used for? Where are they used? Apply this technique to a pen, a cookie, and a brick.

ANSWERS & INTERPRETATIONS

If you generated less than 30 ideas or were not able to arrive at three usable ideas—you have average idea-generation ability. You may have found it hard to be freewheeling in your thinking. Suspending judgment is the most common stumbling block to creative thinking. Remind yourself that you will be able to evaluate later, but now is the time for creative thinking.

If you generated 30 ideas within the time given and arrived at three usable ideas—you have excellent idea-generation ability. You are able to control your thinking and suspend evaluation. This is invaluable for communicating with others and for problem-solving. Being able to listen to the whole story before passing judgment makes you a great people manager.

Can you remember details?

Creative intelligence plays a pivotal role in problem-solving as it enables the generation of ideas to flow unhindered. Creativity also contributes greatly to memory as imagination can be used to create links between significant pieces of information. The more strongly you can imagine and visualize a situation, the more effectively it will stick in your mind for later retrieval. People with good memories use creativity techniques to develop such links and can effortlessly remember shopping lists, birthdays, diary dates, and telephone numbers.

One of the memory games used in boy scout camps is Kim's game, based on an event in Rudyard Kipling's book, *Kim* (1901). Kim becomes friends with a jewelry and antiques merchant, who teaches him how to pay attention to and remember small details. The dealer uncovers a tray full of jewels and asks Kim to look at them for just one minute before he covers them up again. Kim then has to recall as much information about these objects as possible. This game helps develop creative intelligence.

TEST YOUR ABILITY

You will need a stopwatch, a pen, and paper. Look at the objects on the opposite page. Imagine you had to remember them all, just as if you were playing Kim's game. Make a list of the techniques you could use to create links and memory prompts between objects which would help you to remember them.

Boosting tip

Make a list of the types of information that you find difficult to remember: phone numbers, zip codes, bank account numbers. Pick a number that you really want to remember by heart, because it annoys you to keep having to look it up. Choose a creative technique for deriving and remembering it. Keep it in your memory by reciting the derivation every day.

ANSWERS & INTERPRETATIONS

Here are a few suggestions:

* ***By color (for example, three orange items: an orange, a pencil, and a cup).***
* ***By visualizing their position on the tray and drawing on your spatial ability.***
* ***By creating a story around all 10 items (for example, a man entered a café, undid the buttons on his coat, sat down, and ordered a cup of orange-flavored coffee, etc.).***
* ***By imagining all the objects in your house (for example, a cup, spoon, and egg timer in the kitchen, etc).***
* ***By creating an acronym (for example, the initial letters of the items B–C–S–E–O–K–B–P–D–E could make "bb spocked").***
* ***By creating numerical associations (for example, a ball is round like a zero, a pencil looks like a number one, the handle on a cup is like a number two, etc).***
* ***By imagining each object somewhere along your journey into work (for example, you open a door with the key; the egg timer on the doorstep reminds you that you have 20 minutes to get to work; you eat an orange while waiting for the bus, etc).***

If you came up with 4 or less links—you have average creative intelligence, and found it difficult to see beyond the functions of the objects. Develop your creative intelligence by challenging the labels you put on things. Avoid "concrete" thinking.

If you came up with 5 or more links—you have excellent creative intelligence, and enjoyed coming up with possible links and ways of remembering the objects by creating diverse relationships between them. You may have subconsciously brainstormed to arrive at the different responses.

Do you have perfect musical pitch?

SOUND IS ENERGY in the form of vibrations called sound waves. Pitch is the highness or lowness of the note. When a string is plucked, it quivers, which causes the air around it to vibrate, too. These vibrations are picked up by the ear and the brain interprets them as sound. If the vibration is steady, we hear it as a musical note—if it vibrates quickly, we hear a high note, or pitch; if it reverberates slowly, we hear a low note. Pitch dictates where a note sits on the musical scale, a method used to organize notes in order of pitch. Western scales have eight notes, called an octave. The interval between notes differs around the world: the quivering feel of Indian and Chinese music means the interval between notes is much shorter than in Western music, for example. Some people have an innate ability, known as "perfect pitch," to recognize or sing a given note without having to refer to any other pitch. Mozart was able to replicate melodies on the piano just from listening to them once. Conversely, people who are tone deaf cannot tell the difference between notes. The majority of us fall between these two camps: with practice, nearly everyone can learn to distinguish between pitch quite competently.

TEST YOUR ABILITY

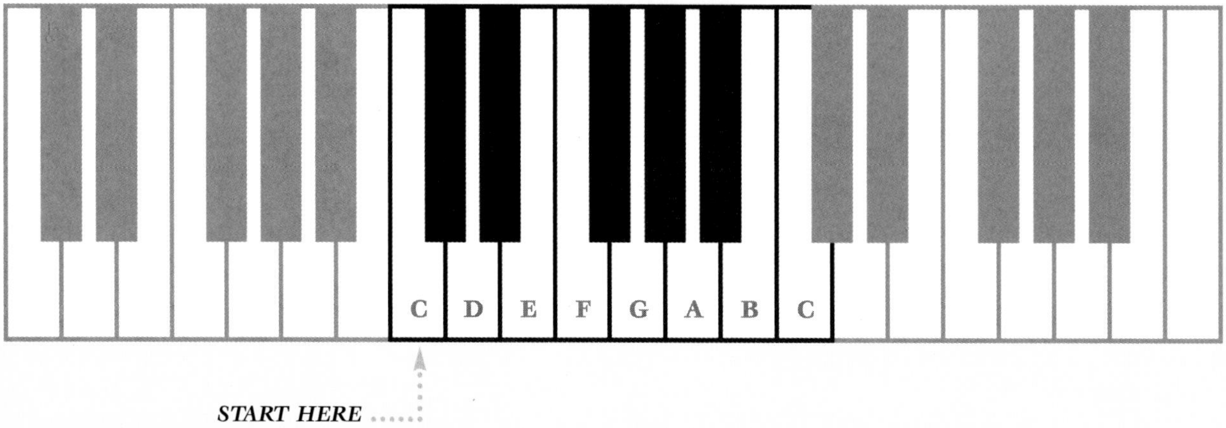

Boosting tips

1. Take five different drinking glasses and fill them up with varying amounts of water. Tap the rim of each with a spoon. Arrange them in order of pitch—from the lowest to the highest.

2. Using the same five glasses, try to sing the note that each produces when you strike it. Ask a friend to evaluate your efforts.

3. Tune into the vibrations in the environment around you. Feel them resound through your body as you hear them. Place them on your own "Richter Scale." How did a bus sound as it rumbled past your building? Could you feel the vibrations from a car with the radio on full blast? What about workers drilling on the sidewalk? Can you feel these sounds?

ANSWERS & INTERPRETATIONS

If you identified all notes correctly, you have excellent pitch, find it easy to detect small changes in pitch, and may have had musical training as a child. You can detect and use pitch in speech to understand or convey your emotions.

If you identified any notes incorrectly, you have average pitch, and probably found it difficult to hear the subtle differences between notes. Develop this by noticing the pitch of your voice when talking to others.

TEST 1

The correct order is: C–C–G–G–A–A–G.

TEST 2

Correct answers will depend on your partner's selection.

You will need a piano or an electric organ for both tests. Test 1 you do alone, test 2 with a partner.

TEST 1

Starting with C, work out the first seven notes of *Twinkle, Twinkle, Little Star*. Make a note of the final order by letter (i.e. C—...).

TEST 2

Sit with your back to the keyboard. Ask your partner to play you a target note. Three seconds later, ask him or her to play you another—either the same note, or the key to the left or right of the first note. Repeat this until you have guessed whether five notes are the same or different. Observe how many you correctly identified.

Have you got rhythm?

Rhythm, together with pitch, constitutes the essence of music and is its heartbeat. It can be generated from striking a single drum, for example, so that the pitch remains constant; it is impossible, however, to have music with pitch and no rhythm. Rhythm is the pulse, what you tap your foot to; it measures the time throughout a piece. In popular music, rhythm is often marked by a drumbeat.

Just as rhythm is central to music, so a feel for rhythm is central to musical intelligence. People with this ability walk gracefully arm-in-arm with a partner, and synchronize with the other person's body rhythm. Dancing to music, either with friends or with a partner, feels natural and easy. From this point of view, musical intelligence has great social advantages.

TEST YOUR SENSE OF RHYTHM

Sit at a table or desk with a partner. Have a pen and paper to hand.

Test 1

Give your partner a list of 10 tunes that you both know. Choose pieces from well-known musicals, popular music, nursery rhymes, or jazz—*She'll Be Coming Round the Mountain*, *Frosty the Snowman*, *Baa Baa Black Sheep*, *Do-Re-Mi* from *The Sound of Music* or *The Star-Spangled Banner*, for example.

Choose five songs from this list, without informing your partner of your choices. For each tune, tap out the beat on the table with your fingers. Get your partner to guess what it is. You may repeat it once. Make a note of how many songs your partner correctly guessed.

Test 2

Sitting at a table or desk with a partner, ask him or her to tap out a rhythm on the table. It can be a tune that he or she knows, or just a replicable beat. You must duplicate the rhythm exactly as you've heard it. Ask your partner to generate a total of five rhythms. Get your partner to judge how many you successfully replicated after just one hearing and note them down.

ANSWERS & INTERPRETATIONS

If your score was 3 or less—you have an average sense of rhythm. You probably found it hard to keep the beats in your head and to translate a beat into your tapping hand. You may enjoy dancing, but would admit it wasn't your main strength! You don't tend to feel the rhythm in music, but you could develop this by watching the sway of dancers, or by honing in on the drumbeat of a piece.

If your score was 4 or more—you have an excellent sense of rhythm. You probably found it relatively easy to translate the beat you felt or imagined into hand or finger movement. You are good at dancing, and often find yourself tapping your foot to a song or a tune that you particularly like to find the beat.

Boosting tip

Notice how the rhythm in music can affect your mood and alternately make you feel energized, lethargic, sad, or uplifted. Choose a selection of music from home, and listen to it on a Walkman or a Discman on the way to work. Listen to a particular track and try to find the beat by tapping your finger on your thigh, or your foot on the ground.

Do you connect with the natural world?

NATURALISTIC INTELLIGENCE was recognized by Howard Gardner in 1995. He described it as the ability to recognize plants, animals, and other elements of the natural world (like rocks, fossils, or clouds) and to see patterns and connections between them. People with this kind of intelligence are acutely aware of their surroundings and changes in the environment. They have highly developed sensory perception, often noticing things that others are unable to tap into. Many tribal people, for example the Australian Aborigines and Native American Indians, possess and greatly value naturalistic intelligence. Charles Darwin, author of *The Origin of the Species* (1859), possessed this intelligence in abundance.

An empathy with nature is usually coupled with an ability to sort and categorize biological and geological specimens so it is understandable that nature-smart individuals enjoyed collecting objects like feathers, leaves, or shells as children. These youngsters have a strong connection with the natural world (evident from their affinity with animals or plants) and a love of nature books or documentaries.

TEST YOURSELF

Decide whether each statement is true (2 points), partly true (1 point), or not true (0 points). Total the number of points.

1. I like animals and can usually get them to trust me.
2. I love being outdoors and going hiking or camping.
3. I have strong sensory skills—taste, touch, sight, hearing, and smell.
4. I notice things about the weather like cloud formations or wind directions.
5. I like to watch and understand natural events like star-gazing or the motion of the tides.
6. I like nurturing plants and could be described as having a "green thumb."
7. I notice patterns in my surroundings—changes, differences, similarities, and connections.
8. I like collecting natural artifacts, or collating facts about natural objects and events.
9. I love watching natural history shows on TV, or reading books and magazines about nature and wildlife.
10. I care about the environment.

ANSWERS & INTERPRETATIONS

If you scored 12 points or less—you have average naturalistic intelligence and probably feel that nature isn't all that relevant to your life. You may have a specific interest in it through owning and looking after a pet, for example, but do not have a global affinity. Try to develop this skill by noticing the weather, animals, and plants around you.

If you scored 13 points of more—you have excellent naturalistic intelligence and an affinity with nature, which probably started in childhood. You see yourself as part of a wider natural world and care deeply about animals, plants, and the environment.

Boosting tips

1. Create a scrapbook about natural objects that appeal to you. For example, you may wish to include observations about the types of birdsong that you hear on your way to work, drawings of unusual cloud shapes, photographs of rock formations, or specimens of beautiful fall leaves.

2. Learn to identify the types of flowers and trees in your back yard or neighborhood. Buy or borrow a book to help you name them.

3. Go to your local park and scan the ground for insects, turning over rocks or stones if necessary. Observe what is happening at ground level. Do they work alone or in groups? Do they like light or shade? Is there a pattern in their movements?

Can you help the environment?

Our ancestors used their affinity with, and knowledge of, their environment to hunt and farm. In the 19th and 20th centuries, as biological and medical research advanced, this was expressed through the numerous man-made methods used to influence and control nature through fertilizers, antibiotics, and disease-resistant crops.

The ability to harness nature, and use it to help humankind, is one of the fruits of naturalistic intelligence. The outcome may be vital to life in the form of food or medicine. We must always be fully aware that we don't own, and are only temporarily sharing, this planet—something nature smart people instinctively understand and respect.

TEST YOURSELF

Imagine you are creating a pond for your back yard or garden, with the aim of attracting local wildlife for you to observe and enjoy. Place the following activities in the order in which you would choose to undertake them. Break activities up into planning, construction, and populating.

A. Install a pump and filter to ensure oxygenated water is available for fish.

B. Introduce a healthy micro-ecosystem by collecting a bucket of water from a clean, nearby pond.

C. Walk around the site and draw a diagram of the relevant landscape features including the house, trees, and any hedge boundaries.

D. Measure for the lining of the pond, cover its base with sand, and line its edges with plastic sheeting.

E. Check local regulations for pond installation and apply for any necessary permits.

F. Stock the pond with native fish.

G. Fill the pond with water by placing the hose in the center of the liner. Allow it to settle for a day or two before trimming the liner and securing the edges with large stones.

H. Mark out the shape of the pond, then dig it, checking that the edges are level. Allow a shelf around the perimeter and a muddy, shallow area for birds and insects.

Boosting tips

1. Take a walk in the park and spend a few minutes observing what is going on around you. How does the wind move through the trees? What are the birds busy doing? Can you spot any insects in the grass? Which plants are flourishing at this time of year?

2. Regularly watch *National Geographic*, *The Discovery Channel*, and other TV programs to learn more about wildlife here and elsewhere.

I. Plant a mix of native plants: some submerged (to oxygenate the water), some floating (as a habitat for wildlife), and marginal plants around the pond (to create a barrier against land predators like cats).

J. Decide on the best location and shape of the pond, bearing in mind that, although aquatic plants need plenty of daily sunshine, excessive sunlight causes algal growth on the surface of the water. Ensure there is a route for wildlife to travel safely to and from the pond (i.e. through tall grass or reeds).

ANSWERS & INTERPRETATIONS

The correct order is:

***Planning:* E–C–J**

***Construction:* H–D–G–A**

***Populating:* I–B–F**

Planning and construction ensures that you consider and create all the necessary factors for attracting and maintaining a healthy pond for plants and animals. Populating the pond takes into account the needs of, and relationship between, plants and animals.

If you placed all the activities in the correct order, you have excellent applied naturalistic intelligence. You are in tune with nature and are able to manage it to your advantage. You probably enjoy gardening, keeping pets, and being outdoors. You may also be a collector.

If you placed the activities in any other order, you have average applied naturalistic intelligence. You probably would not undertake a task like this in real life. Try to enhance your ability by caring for a pet or house plants.

Do you have intuition?

Generally speaking, there are three ways in which we use our brains to survive in the world that surrounds us: firstly, through instinct, which is specific to our species and is something we are all born with; secondly, through intelligence, the ability to think consciously; thirdly, through intuition, the deep-seated ability to learn and process information subconsciously. This underlies those times when the right answer to a complex problem pops into your head, or when your brain picks up patterns in a seemingly chaotic situation.

Children learn primarily through intuition—they don't yet have the ability to think logically or rationally. For example, they pick up language and speech through "absorption," without having any understanding of grammar.

Individuals with strong intuitive intelligence form impressions about events that lack details and can see the bigger picture. They are adept at coming up with ideas, concepts, and relationships that others miss, because they have a sense of what to try next.

TEST YOURSELF

Read each statement below and decide whether it is never true (0 points), partly or sometimes true (1 point), or always true (2 points). Add up your total score.

- I sometimes delay making a decision because I know the right course of action will eventually become clear.
- I get feelings about things that later prove to be correct.
- I can usually guess what will happen in a book or movie by the time I'm halfway through it.
- I tend not to rely on written instructions for gadgets because I establish how to operate them through trial and error.
- I read between the lines of what people write or say to arrive at an alternative view.
- I can work things out without being able to explain how I arrived at an answer.
- I am interested in things that are new or different.
- I believe in taking a leap of faith with certain, specific situations.
- I can sense if two people are in a relationship, even if it is a secret.
- I trust my gut instinct when I meet someone for the first time.

ANSWERS & INTERPRETATIONS

If you scored 12 points or less—you have average intuitive intelligence. You may pick up on things around you, but don't always see the overall picture. Develop your intuitive intelligence by taking a leap of faith and trusting your inner judgment.

If you scored 13 points or more—you have excellent intuitive intelligence. You pick up clues and ideas and store them in your subconscious until a pattern emerges. Your ability to process complex information without conscious effort is an underrated talent.

Boosting tips

1. Postpone a decision for one day. Write down what you would have done if you had acted immediately. Write down what you decide to do after 24 hours, having allowed the intuitive side of your brain a chance to process the facts. What new insights did you find? What had your conscious mind overlooked that your subconscious remembered?

2. Have fun with your intuition. Think of a colleague and write down three predictions: what he or she will wear tomorrow, how many cups of coffee he or she will drink, and the time he or she will leave the office at the end of the day. Check your predictions for accuracy. What thought processes did you go through to arrive at your predictions?

How do you obtain information?

Carl Jung (1875–1961), a Swiss psychiatrist and a friend of Sigmund Freud, tried to understand and explain individual differences in people, including introverts and extroverts. Whichever type we are, we still have to deal with the world both inwardly and outwardly. Jung coined the word "sensing" for those individuals who obtain information from the world mainly through their senses by observing and listening (the predominant thinking style in Western philosophy). Jung reserved the term "intuition" for those individuals who notice what is going on inside of themselves, are more introspective, and primarily listen to their inner voices. Intuiting derives from the complex integration of large amounts of information, rather than just what the senses detect. People with a preference for intuition prefer to gain understanding through insight rather than hands-on experience. Jung believed that individuals tend to be *either* sensing *or* intuitive—that one is dominant while the other is repressed—but that we should strive to be both. His work provided the basis for the famous Myers-Briggs Type Indicator® instrument, one of the most widely used tools for understanding normal personality differences.

TEST YOURSELF

Choose the answers that best describe you.

1. I work from...

a) the bigger picture first, then gradually get down to the facts.

b) the facts first, which I then gradually piece together into the bigger picture.

2. I solve problems...

a) through insight, leaps of faith, and a feeling that I have identified the "right" thing to do.

b) by working through things thoroughly until I have a complete understanding.

3. I remember events...

a) as an overall impression or an essence of what has occurred.

b) as the literal words or experiences of what has unfolded.

4. I sometimes...

a) focus so much on new possibilities that I forget to consider the practicalities.

b) concentrate so much on the facts that I miss new possibilities.

ANSWERS & INTERPRETATIONS

Mostly a's—you are an intuitive type and tend to be concerned with what is possible, new, and the future. You probably enjoy working in abstract or theoretical terms and are quite creative. You don't mind if new ideas don't have an obvious application and are more likely to adopt new technology. You like to know your destination, but don't worry about how you will get there.

Mostly b's—you are a sensing type, are in tune with everyday physical reality and experience, and tend to be concerned with what is actual, present, current, and real. You probably have a great memory for detail, an eye for facts, and are good at sorting out the practical aspects of problems. You would want to know the route to your destination.

5. I am...

a) interested in doing things that are new and different.

b) interested in doing things that are practical and pragmatic.

6. I am more interested in...

a) the future and its possibilities.

b) the present and its realities.

Boosting tips

1. If you are a sensing type, boost your intuition by focusing on the future—you can't experience it and there are no facts or details to distract you. Make a plan of where you want to be in one year's time, professionally and personally. Note down an event and a corresponding emotion (i.e. "will change jobs—anxious," or "will move apartment—excited").

2. Everyone experiences intuition differently—as the tingling of skin; a sinking feeling in the stomach; inner voices; irrational attractions or aversions to people you've just met; sudden, inspirational solutions; and mental imagery. Record each time one of these sensations occurs and what it means to you.

Your creative intelligence

NOW THAT YOU'VE completed all the creative intelligence tests, you can profile your results to get an overall view of your strengths. Check the relevant boxes for each of your test profiles.

- If you have the most number of checks in the average column, you have adequate-to-good creative intelligence and prefer logical and linear thinking.
- If you have the most number of checks in the excellent column, you possess superior creative intelligence. You favor creative over lateral thinking.

	Average ✓	*Excellent* ✓
Test 1 (pages 164-65)		
Test 2 (pages 166-67)		
Test 3 (pages 168-69)		

Developing and improving creative intelligence

Being able to separate divergent and convergent thinking enables you to apply each exclusively at the appropriate point in the decision-making process. Suspend your judgment and generate lots of ideas, so you can then re-activate judgment and evaluate them. Good problem-solving comes up with as many solutions to choose from as possible.

If you have adequate-to-good creative intelligence, be careful not to smother the generation of ideas by layering your values and impressions on what will or won't work. This kills creativity.

If you possess superior creative intelligence, try to encourage others to think creatively, too. At work, set time aside with your colleagues, for example, to show them the ropes and help them brainstorm.

Working with children

Although youngsters are naturally creative, the educational process favors logical thinking. Creative and imaginative play (painting or dressing up, for example) are crucial first steps in allowing children free rein. Once they are old enough, and are starting to learn about deduction and cause and effect, try introducing creative thought. You could, for instance, awaken creativity by:

- Discussing options to develop the generation of ideas. How many different types of toys are there? What are the different ways that people can travel?
- Encouraging them to think and act independently (within the limits of rules and safety). Spend a day with a child and allow him or her to dictate what you do and where you go.
- Asking children how they would prepare a meal without electricity, pots, pans, or a fridge.
- Exposing children to many diverse cultures and communities, so they can appreciate that there are many different ways of behaving and living. If you live in a city, try a visit to Chinatown; if you live in the country, visit a specialized farming comunity.

Your musical intelligence

HAVING COMPLETED THE TESTS, you probably already have a good feel for your musical intelligence. See if your impression is correct by checking the revelant boxes to reveal your profile.

- If you have 1-2 checks in the average column, you have adequate-to-good musical intelligence. You are likely to enjoy music purely on an emotional level rather than a technical level.
- If you have 2 checks in the excellent column, you have superior musical intelligence. You are likely to enjoy all aspects of music, emotional and technical, and may even compose your own pieces.

	Average ✓	*Excellent* ✓
Test 1 (pages 170-71)		
Test 2 (pages 172-73)		

Developing and improving musical intelligence

Musical education is related to improvements in spatial and logical abilities. Schools in Hungary, for example, which incorporate extensive musical education from kindergarten upward, have students who outperform other countries in science subjects.

If you have adequate-to-good musical intelligence, decide whether you most want to improve pitch or rhythm. Practice listening to sounds, identifying them, and then reproducing them to develop your pitch. You can also buy a tuning fork, learn that note, and listen out for it in different types of music. Develop your sense of rhythm by becoming more aware of it: listen to music and focus on the beat; get into the habit of tapping it out with your hand or foot.

If you have superior musical intelligence, are you applying it to all areas of your life? If you enjoy listening to music, try singing, or taking up a musical instrument. If you already play an instrument, try composing your own songs or music. If you already compose, explore the possibility of earning a living from your talent.

Working with children

Children love making and listening to music. Young children enjoy nursery rhymes and clapping to a beat. Older children like dancing and playing simple tunes. You could, for instance, really help encourage musical aptitude by:

- Making your own musical instruments. Use cereal boxes for drums; empty kleenex boxes strung with rubber bands for guitars; rocks or buttons inside tin boxes for shakers.
- Showing children that they can produce different sounds with their body. Clap your hands, snap your fingers, slap your thighs, and stomp your feet.
- Encouraging children to listen to and make up songs to remember things like numbers and letters.

Your naturalistic intelligence

Hopefully you've enjoyed discovering more about your naturalistic intelligence. By checking the relevant boxes for both of these tests, you will discover an overview of your strengths in this area.

- If you have 1-2 checks in the average column, you have adequate-to-good naturalistic intelligence. You enjoy nature for its beauty, rather than trying to comprehend or classify it.
- If you have 2 checks in the excellent column, you have superior naturalistic intelligence. You are likely to have a job or a hobby that includes your love and understanding of nature.

	Average ✓	*Excellent* ✓
***Test 1* (pages 174-75)**		
***Test 2* (pages 176-77)**		

Developing and improving naturalistic intelligence

One of the misconceptions about nature and science is that it's only about answers—in fact, it's also about asking questions. People with naturalistic intelligence observe and question. This is linked to logical intelligence, since the ability to sort and classify is a component of logical thought.

If you possess average-to-good naturalistic intelligence, learn to ask questions. Your curiosity is key to getting in tune with nature. Think about and research topics you have always wondered about but never understood. Why are clouds different shapes? Why is there snow on the top of mountains? Why do birds sing?

If you have superior naturalistic intelligence, you probably loved nature from an early age. Consider whether you still get a buzz from it, the way you did as a child. Bring some of that joy back into your life. Buy (or look after) a pet, a window box, or simply nurture your garden or back yard. A career involving the natural world might even be a viable option.

Working with children

Youngsters have a great empathy with nature and love being outdoors. Turn a mundane trip to the store into a rich, learning experience by drawing their attention to the weather, the environment, and the living things around them. You could, for instance, develop their naturalistic intelligence by:

- Keeping a diary and comparing the actual weather with the TV forecasts.
- Putting a white tulip or daffodil into water with food coloring and observing how the dye travels up the stem and into the petals.
- Visiting science museums, nature reserves, or national parks.
- Going on nature walks and writing down all the insects and bugs that you spot together.
- Making a scrapbook collection of leaves or flowers. Identify the names of the plants they came from together, and write these down next to each specimen.

Your intuitive intelligence

PROFILING YOUR INTUITIVE intelligence will give you insights into how you currently use this skill, and may give you ideas for how to develop it in the future. Profile your test results by checking the relevant boxes on this page.

- If you have 1-2 checks in the average column, you possess adequate-to-good intuitive intelligence. You are likely to be more of a practical person, someone who focuses on detail and fact.
- If you have 2 checks in the excellent column, you have superior intuitive intelligence. You are likely to be a "possibilities" person, someone who focuses on the bigger picture.

	Average ✓	*Excellent* ✓
***Test 1* (pages 178-79)**		
***Test 2* (pages 180-81)**		

Developing and improving intuitive intelligence

Intuition is an extremely valuable tool. Until recently, it was rather downplayed as lacking substance and hard evidence. Learn to strengthen your natural intuition so that it comes to mind more readily, but remember that you cannot "make" it work because it lies deep in your subconscious.

If you have adequate-to-good intuitive intelligence, your strengths probably lie in thinking logically and practically, so learn to give your subconscious time and space to sift through the data that your brain has stored. Allow yourself at least a day to mull over a situation, then formulate a plan, and decide on your course of action.

If you have superior intuitive intelligence, make sure you are applying it in your personal and professional life. There are times when business decisions and relationships can be informed by your intuition, just as there are times when your private choices and relationships may benefit from a more intuitive way of thinking.

Working with children

Youngsters are naturally intuitive because their logical reasoning is still in its infancy. You can ensure this innate ability stays with them throughout their lives by nurturing and valuing intuitive thought, which can be forgotten in an educational environment that focuses on logical deduction. You could, for instance, develop their intuitive intelligence by:

- Focusing on the whole picture rather than the detail. Discuss your plans and aims for the day with your kids, rather than just bundling them into a car in the morning.
- Not dismissing children's gut feelings, likes, and dislikes of people. Tease out their thought processes and the reasons for them.
- Giving children thinking time before asking them to make a decision. Get them to sleep on it and explain how their brain is subconsciously trying to sort things out for them.

What is your learning style?

One of the most remarkable and useful features of applying multiple intelligence theory to adult learning and development is its identification of an individual's cognitive and physical strengths through his or her preferred learning style. Are you in a job you feel isn't bringing out your strengths? Do you find it difficult to concentrate? Do you find yourself having to interpret what others say when they are explaining something to you? Then you're working in an information format (written or verbal) that doesn't reflect your learning style of choice. Discover what your style is and begin to adjust and arrange information in the way your brain is most receptive to it so you are able to retain more material.

Learning styles represent different ways of remembering information. You may find that these work in combination with, or complement, other styles: for example, musically inclined individuals might also be naturally pre-disposed toward a numerical learning style.

Sixty percent of the population displays a linguistic learning style. Such individuals are largely visual learners and relate most effectively to written information, notes, diagrams, and pictures, and will take notes even with printed material before them. They need to sit at the front of a class and see the teacher's body language and facial expressions to take in the content of what is being taught. Chances are that you'll be in this category but do the test opposite and discover your learning style of choice.

TEST YOURSELF

Check those statements that most apply to you.

- ☐ **1.** I like to do things in a systematic way.
- ☐ **2.** I find mental arithmetic easy.
- ☐ **3.** I love doing crosswords.
- ☐ **4.** I am frequently a peacemaker in arguments between friends.
- ☐ **5.** I am able to control my moods.
- ☐ **6.** I tend to fidget and am always moving about.
- ☐ **7.** I use music to express feelings.

- ☐ **1.** I often draw diagrams to explain things.
- ☐ **2.** I like to put figures to facts.
- ☐ **3.** I learn a lot from talks, lectures, and presentations.
- ☐ **4.** I enjoy group activities and sports.
- ☐ **5.** I know myself pretty well.
- ☐ **6.** I learn best by doing, trying, or acting things out.
- ☐ **7.** I often have a tune in my head.

- ☐ **1.** I enjoy jigsaws, computer games, and solving logical problems.
- ☐ **2.** I like mathematical problems, puzzles, and "brain-teasers."

- 3. I find it easy to express myself in writing.
- 4. I am good at talking people into things.
- 5. I quite like my own company.
- 6. I mimic other people's facial expressions, gestures, and mannerisms.
- 7. I tap my feet or hands when I hear music.

- 1. I have a good sense of direction.
- 2. I follow the fluctuations of the stock market.
- 3. I enjoy discussions and debates.
- 4. I am the person others turn to for advice.
- 5. I like working alone, with time to reflect.
- 6. I tend to touch people whenever I'm in deep conversation with them.
- 7. I detect when someone is singing off-key.

Note down the question number beside each check. Total your checks for each type.

Total number of 1s____conceptual intelligence
Total number of 2s____numerical intelligence
Total number of 3s____linguistic intelligence
Total number of 4s____emotional intelligence
Total number of 5s____personal intelligence
Total number of 6s____physical intelligence
Total number of 7s____musical intelligence

PROFILE INTERPRETATIONS

*If most of your checks were 1s, your preferred learning style is **conceptual**. You learn best by identifying patterns and relationships, classifying, sorting, and working with pictures and charts. Map out what you want to learn in a logical diagram.*

*If most of your checks were 2s, your preferred learning style is **numerical**. You learn best in numerical formats by counting and comparing data. Convert what you want to learn into numbers.*

*If most of your checks were 3s, your preferred learning style is **linguistic**. You learn best by seeing, reading, speaking, writing, and hearing. Record what you want to learn on tape and play it back in the car.*

*If most of your checks were 4s, your preferred learning style is **emotional**. You learn best in a group setting by sharing information, interviewing, and debating. Join an evening class or study group.*

*If most of your checks were 5s, your preferred learning style is **personal**. You learn best by working alone, in your own personal space, using reflection and self-analysis. Do a correspondence course, where you can work at your given pace.*

*If most of your checks were 6s, your preferred learning style is **physical**. You learn best through touch, movement, and acting things out. Silently act out what you want to learn, where applicable.*

*If most of your checks were 7s, your preferred learning style is **musical**. You learn best when listening to music, rhythm, melody, and singing. Play background music while you study or make up songs about the things you wish to remember.*

More on tests and testing

TESTING IS CERTAINLY on the increase, particularly in countries like the United States. It is fairly common now for you (or your children) to be asked to take a test at school or at work, or you may simply decide to test yourself out of interest—the reason why you picked up this book in the first place! It is therefore important that you are aware of who is using tests, the reasons why, the types of tests out there, and ways of improving your chances of success.

Who uses tests and why

It is now common practice for organizations to use psychological tests as a way of finding out more about potential or current employees. Tests provide a level playing field by which everyone's performance can be compared. Every candidate is unique, yet there will be similarities and these may have important practical consequences. If you are employing people to input data into a computer, for example, you will be looking primarily for fast and accurate hand-eye coordination. If you are recruiting new senior managers, however, your considerations will include a whole host of factors such as good people skills, numeracy, and verbal aptitude.

Tests are also used in schools and colleges to screen and assess students. These tools may initially form part of a selection process, but they can then be applied to helping allocate the appropriate classes to specific students, and may later be used for monitoring purposes. Tests are useful in career guidance to help students understand their own strengths and weaknesses, so they are able to make reasoned choices about which profession to follow.

In common with career-guidance testing, tests are applied to promote adult self-understanding and awareness. You want to know why you find some things easier to do than others, why you prefer to work or learn in a certain way, and where your hidden talents lie, so you can maximize them.

Types of tests

Test results are used to inform life-changing decisions. You should expect these professional tests to meet the exacting standards of any other professional tool. If you were having an operation, for example, you would expect the surgeon's scalpel to have a sharper blade than your kitchen knife at home. There are standard methods of gauging just how sophisticated testing methods actually are, and tests that reach these exacting standards are called professional psychological tests. These should be the only tests to be professionally used in schools, colleges, and organizations because they have been proven to be valid (accurately measuring what they purport to measure), reliable (results are dependable and stable over time), and fair (tests do not discriminate against any gender, race, or creed).

Every country has a professional body of psychologists that governs the use and distribution of such tests. In the United States, this is the American Psychological Association (APA). The APA has strict guidelines about the sale, use, and interpretation of psychological tests. The general public cannot buy or be granted access to these tests because their administration and interpretation requires specialist psychological training. This restriction also ensures that no candidate has seen the items before the testing session begins.

There are four main types of tests which are currently used in education and by organizations:

- Personality tests designed to gauge personality preferences and tendencies;
- Aptitude tests designed to ascertain the potential for developing particular skills;
- Ability tests designed to determine specific skills and strengths;
- Achievement tests designed to measure scholastic aptitude and academic brilliance.

IMPROVING YOUR CHANCES OF SUCCESS

For the best results, it is really important that your test scores accurately reflect **you**. *Here's some advice on how to get the most from tests:*

1. Practice in advance the type of tests you will be asked to take.

2. Eat and sleep well before the test to give you energy and a rested mind.

3. Read questions carefully. Make sure you understand what is being asked before attempting an answer. If example questions are available, ask the examiner for help if you don't understand a particular item.

4. Some tests penalize wrong answers, which will be stipulated in the instructions. In these tests, power rather than speed is being assessed. Build in extra time to review all your answers toward the end of the time limit.

5. Some questions are deliberately difficult! Skip over them, moving on to an easier question. Return to the challenging items at the very end.

6. If you are answering questions about your preferences in a personality test, be honest with yourself. People who thrive in a job do so because their personality genuinely fits in with the organization's values and the requirements of the job. There's no point in pretending. You're only fooling yourself!

7. Do ask for your results since examiners are ethically required to give you feedback.

Index

A—C

D—G

H—K

T—Z

Acknowledgments

The author would like to thank:

Dr Kirsty Smedley, clinical psychologist. Her extensive knowledge of psychological assessment and intelligence and her professional advice were invaluable. She also happens to be my sister. My family and friends for freeing up my time to write; my husband, Chris; my parents, Maggie and Sean; Pat and Tom; Kathryn and David; Sophie and Chris; Pete and Emma; and Sue.

Chris A—I hope your faith is justified.

And, finally, the team at Carroll & Brown:
My dedicated and talented editor, ***Anna Amari-Parker***; ***Amy Carroll***, for steering the book so skillfully; ***Frank Cawley***, for directing the elegant design and illustration; and ***Bala Tharan***, for his insights into numerical intelligence.

Carroll & Brown would like to thank:

Editorial assistance
Tom Broder, ***Stuart Moorhouse***

Illustrations
(Chapters 1 and 2) ***Jim Cheatle***
(Chapter 3) ***Neil A Webb at début art***
(Chapter 4) ***Jacey at début art***
(Chapter 5 and 6) ***Frank Cawley***
(Chapter 7) ***Frank Cawley/Neil A Webb***
(Paper sculptures) ***Gail Armstrong at Illustration***

Illustration of the human brain on pp6-7 © Reader's Digest Association

Production
Karol Davies, ***Nigel Reed***

IT
Paul Stradling

Photography
Jules Selmes

Index
Richard Bird